Praise for
Stick Like Glue
How to Create an Everlasting *Bond* ..... Your Customers
So They Spend More, Stay Longer, and Refer More!

This is a FUN book to read. Jim's personality not only shines in this book, but he delivers the "must-read business book of 2010." If you are an entrepreneur or own a business, you need to get this book and follow all of Jim's recommendations.... I have, and was shocked at how my customers responded. Referrals are THOUGH the roof!

—Brian Horn
www.BeOnPage1ofGoogle.com

Jim's advice on customer retention over the past six years has been instrumental in growing my company from a three-person start-up to a multi-million-dollar operation with over 300 corporate clients, in less than three years—even in a challenging marketplace. Keeping profitable customers happy has done more for my own peace of mind than any other business practice. Protect your most valuable asset—your best customers—and teach your employees to do the same. Live by the words in *Stick Like Glue*!

—Bobby Deraco,
CEO & Founder
www.SynapseResults.com

If you're looking for how to create an everlasting bond with your customers so they spend more, stay longer, and refer more, then I recommend Jim's book, *Stick Like Glue*. This is head and shoulders one of the most important business books I've read this year, and I recommend it for every entrepreneur, especially during a difficult economy. Jim has the knowledge, understanding, and experience to guide you through what you should do, and, importantly, what you shouldn't do, to improve your business. Not only is he the "Newsletter Guru," but after reading this book, he should be the "Marketing Guru." This book should be required reading for every small business owner in the country. It's that good.

—Gerry Oginski, Esq.,
Founder, Lawyers Video Studio, LLC
http://LawyersVideoStudio.com

Another great book by Jim Palmer! In his first book, *The Magic of Newsletter Marketing*, Jim explained how to use newsletters to create a strong relationship with your customers. Now, in the same no-fluff conversational style, Jim gives dozens of ideas for keeping the customers you've worked so hard to get. You can trust Jim's advice because it comes from 30 years of working directly with customers. He knows what he's talking about, and the stories he shares prove that his strategies work. The Sticky Notes sprinkled throughout the chapters and summary Sticking Points at the end of each chapter make it easy to find and remember the key points. This is a book you'll refer to often if one of your goals is to keep customers from doing business with your competitors.

—Meredith Bell,
President, Performance Support Systems, Inc.
www.ProStarCoach.com

Jim Palmer is a master of growing businesses and keeping his clients and customers happy and loyal. His most recent book, *Stick Like Glue*, is a goldmine of techniques for growing a loyal customer base and how to make it continually more and more profitable. His first chapter alone on acquisition and retention can make you more money than many weeklong seminars and courses costing thousands of dollars. Want to be richer in every way? Get this book and do one new thing each month. It's that easy with Jim's help.

—Dave Frees
www.SuccessTechnologies.com/blog

Jim Palmer's book *Stick Like Glue* is an amazing resource every business owner needs—whether you're a seasoned veteran, a brand-new business owner, or fall somewhere in between. Referrals are one of the best sources of new business, and if you employ the strategies Jim has laid out for you here, you're almost certain to increase your referrals, and your overall business, in the process (and have a lot of fun doing it). This is a must-read, incredibly valuable resource for anybody looking to get real referrals that will turn into clients who also refer.

—Diane Conklin,
Co-Founder, Complete Marketing Systems, LLC
www.CompleteMarketingSystems.com

I highly recommend Jim Palmer's new book *Stick Like Glue*! EVERYONE should. This fantastic book gives you the blueprint for improving your lead generation, your conversions, and your customer retention. Most definitely a must-have for your business bookshelf. My highest recommendation.

—Troy White,
Responsive Direct Marketing
www.TroysBlog.com

I'd recommend anything Jim Palmer puts his name to. Jim knows what it takes to attract and keep clients coming back over and over again. As Dan Kennedy says, "Retention is the new acquisition," and Jim Palmer is the "retention expert."

—David H. Meir,
The Portrait Expert
www.The-Portrait-Expert.com

Jim Palmer's book *Stick Like Glue: How to Create An Everlasting* Bond *With Your Customers So They Spend More, Stay Longer, and Refer More!* is a terrific and valuable resource that can help business owners, entrepreneurs, and sales professionals retain customers and grow their businesses. I know, because I have been using Jim's services, and he has helped me connect and deepen relationships with my customers and clients.

—Steve Clark,
CEO and Author of *Profitable Persuasion*
www.NewSchoolSelling.com

Jim Palmer has done it again! ANOTHER great book that's easy to read, and, better than that, Jim makes it easy for you to take action! If you're looking for a book that will help you grow your business, look no further, and buy *Stick Like Glue* today!

—Nick Nanton,
The Celebrity Lawyer
www.CelebrityBrandingAgency.com

If you want to know how to get your new customers to keep buying more, and more often, from you for years to come, then you must get and read Jim Palmer's book *Stick Like Glue*. Jim rightly points out how very important it is to your profits to create customers that are "over-the-top" happy with you! Way to go, Jim!

—Adam Urbanski
www.TheMarketingMentors.com

I highly recommend Jim Palmer's book *Stick Like Glue*. It is a great resource that can help even the most seasoned entrepreneur and small business owner get and keep more customers. And it's a fun read!

—Ari Galper,
Founder, Unlock The Game
www.UnlockTheGame.com

Would I recommend Jim Palmer's book? Heck yeah, I would! It's not often that I recommend books to people, but this was such an easy and fun read AND it really delivers results! You won't be disappointed.

—Amy Suzanne Taggart,
CEO, designFORMARE
www.DesignFORMARE.com

Stick Like Glue is the ultimate resource for building and maintaining strong relationships with your customers. Through many examples, Jim displays the genuine approach he's taken over the years to form everlasting bonds with his customers. These tips are sure to *stick* with entrepreneurs and business owners alike.

—Tess Wittler,
Tess Wittler Writing Services
www.TessWittler.com

Once again, Jim Palmer over-delivers—and why wouldn't he? That's what his new book is all about. *Stick Like Glue* is a business plan just waiting to be implemented. I've built my business on many of these same principals over the years, and Jim now presents them in one easy-to-use resource. I urge you to get your highlighter out and start implementing these principles today. Your business will be both more fruitful and more fun if you take action.

—Jay McGrath
www.eLocalMarketing.com

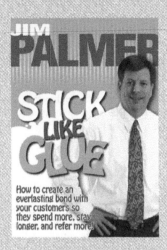

Stick Like Glue

**How to Create an Everlasting *Bond* with
Your Customers So They Spend More,
Stay Longer, and Refer More!**

By Jim Palmer
The Newsletter Guru

With a Foreword by Lee Milteer

CUSTOM NEWSLETTERS, INC.

Stick Like Glue
How to Create an Everlasting *Bond* with Your Customers So They Spend More, Stay Longer, and Refer More!

Published by Success Advantage Publishing
64 East Uwchlan Ave.
P.O. Box 231
Exton, PA 19341

ISBN: 978-0-578-06009-5

Cover design by Jim Saurbaugh, JS Graphic Design - jsgd@verizon.net

This book is dedicated to my family,
Stephanie, Nick, Steve, Jessica, and Amanda

Contents

Foreword

By Lee Milteer

In my career, I have committed myself to lifting people to a new mindset, one that will allow them to take a quantum leap in their lives and businesses. The truth is that everyone is in sales, but average people tend to take the path of least resistance. They don't update their mindsets and skills for success.

When Jim Palmer asked me to write the foreword for *Stick Like Glue*, I was pleased to.

Jim is an unbelievably good man who has a great work ethic and fabulous marketing materials. I met him several years ago when he spoke to my Peak Performers coaching group about the power of newsletters. The audience was on the edge of their seats with the depth of his knowledge about how to market and get noticed by customers.

I am happy to report that Jim not only inspired my entrepreneurial coaching group to stop only "thinking" about doing a newsletter, but after his presentation, more than 80 percent of the room actually started one! The results of Jim's speech helped my group enjoy profits and more business than they ever imagined, because they implemented his advice on using newsletters and different types of marketing strategies.

I even got hooked on Jim's advice. I had played around with doing newsletters, but never really committed to a regular schedule, until I heard Jim speak of the benefits. He emphasized to me that I had been leaving huge profits on the table. When I left that meeting and met with my staff, we created a plan to produce a newsletter every single week. I am thrilled to report that the benefits of his advice have resulted in many new customers and amazing profits for my business.

If you are open to new possibilities, and to new ideas on how to create an everlasting bond with your customers so they spend more, stay longer, and refer you to others more, you are reading the right book!

Jim is not an "Ivory Tower" author. He is someone who has had more than twenty-five years of experience in sales and marketing, and has always exceeded customer expectations. In other words, Jim Palmer knows how to give you the knowledge to cater to your customers, in a way that makes them hyper-responsive, because you give them outstanding service.

The truth is, the more you do for your customers, the more challenging it is for them to walk away from your business. Plus, they will become your best advertising campaign because of their word-of-mouth comments to others.

I promise, if you follow Jim Palmer's advice, you will have dramatic results, and a renewed sense of enthusiasm about the contributions you make to others with your knowledge, products, and services.

In the new reality and economy that we are living in today, knowing how to sell is not enough anymore. Business owners must learn to see life—and our customers—from an entirely different perspective. Value has replaced image, and intrinsic worth has replaced name brands. Our clients are asking themselves very important questions such as:

Does this feel real?   What is good service?
What is quality?   Who can I count on and believe in?

Today's consumers are intelligent, alert, highly selective, and independent in their thinking. To work with today's consumers, you must strive for excellence, integrity, and high ethics. You must be someone that stands out from the competition.

In the new model of selling, you want to focus on sales as a means of creating relationships, not just making deals.

As a business owner, you want to honor your customers, be sensitive to their needs, interests, and desires, and care about what is right for them.

Most traditional sales philosophies are outdated in today's crowded marketplace. The future belongs to the salespeople and organizations that are flexible and nontraditional in their thinking. That is why Jim Palmer's *Stick Like Glue* is an important tool for your future business success.

I am proud to say that Jim Palmer is one of the greatest teachers to provide you with techniques and strategies to take you to an entirely new level of understanding, and success, in your business.

Open yourself to a new level of thinking. Put aside your old opinions and the belief systems that have guided your sales career up to today. Read this book with an open mind, and open heart, and you will find wisdom to transform your business.

Deep down, everyone who owns a business wants to be proud of their work and their contributions. Everyone wants to feel like their work has value and importance to others. The bottom line is that, as a business owner, you are using your life energy and time to contribute to others with your knowledge, products, and services. So why not cut your learning curve, and learn from an expert like Jim Palmer and this new book, *Stick Like Glue*? I promise you, this knowledge will transform your business.

—Lee Milteer
Author of *Success Is an Inside Job* and
Spiritual Power Tools for Successful Selling
www.milteer.com

Preface

"There is only one boss. The customer. And he can fire
everybody in the company from the chairman on down,
simply by spending his money somewhere else."
—Sam Walton

"The single most important thing to remember about
any enterprise is that there are no results inside its walls.
The result of a business is a satisfied customer."
—Peter Drucker

Welcome to what I sincerely hope will be a book that will transform your business. You will not find a lot of classroom theory, business philosophy, or platitudes about what it takes to have happy customers and grow your business. Instead, you will find authentic stories, actual examples, and real-world truths from somebody who has worked the front lines in business for more than twenty-five years in retail, franchise management, association management, and for nearly ten years running my own businesses.

What I'm going to urge you to do in your business has produced dramatic results, not only for my own businesses, but also for my previous employers.

A few quick examples of these results:

- When I was twenty-one, I was promoted to manager of a bike shop. As manager, I grew it from $330K in sales to $960K in less than four years. (At the time, the average bike shop in the United States was grossing approximately $250K.)
- As regional manager, I guided the largest store in the chain (one of the largest bike shops in the country) from $940K to $1.4 million in less than two years.

- As director of franchise operations, I was part of a team that grew a national franchise chain from 14 stores in 2 states to 80 stores in 18 states; I was then recruited to help launch a national marketing association that achieved combined sales of $500 million in less than two years.

- Finally, since starting my first business in the fall of 2001, I've achieved substantial growth by practicing and applying the exact same strategies and principles that I'm going to share in this book. In fact, during the difficult recessionary months of 2009, I more than doubled the size of No Hassle Newsletters (www.NoHassleNewsletters.com), my flagship company. My team and I now serve hundreds of customers in seven countries.

None of this is about bragging or chest pounding. I share some of my accomplishments so that you'll understand the basis for my advice, opinions, and suggestions and know that they've been tested.

Please consider this book a personal conversation between you and me. I not only write in a conversational tone, but I'm also going to give you the straight scoop, as if I were consulting with you. The entrepreneurs whom I coach know me to be candid and blunt, and that's the way it should be, as time is too short for any other approach, especially in this difficult economy.

As the title indicates, this book is about one thing—getting more customers, keeping them longer, selling them more of your products and services, and getting them to refer more new customers to you.

I guarantee that some of what I suggest will require a mindset shift, a small mindset shift for some, and a major overhaul for others! But I also know from nearly thirty years' experience that this stuff truly works. I've seen it work successfully many times, for myself and others.

Let me share a quick story from my time in the franchise business.

I was running a training program for a group of new franchise owners, and one of them, whom I'll call Tom, was a just-retired corporate banker. Tom was a typical buttoned-up executive who spent years in what I refer to as the "Ivory Tower."

At one point in the training program, I began to share some of my "over-the-top" customer service stories (I'll share some with you in this book), when I noticed that Tom had his arms folded across his chest.

I asked, "Everything okay, Tom?"

He said that while he "bought" most of what I was teaching about customer service, he wasn't buying this "give-the-store-away" (his words) mentality, especially when a customer is wrong.

Tom continued, "I totally believe in customer service, Jim, but when customers are right, they're right, and when they're wrong, they're wrong, and I'll do my best to help them out."

Tom clearly had his own strong views, and so I pressed on with the rest of the training.

Tom's first year in business was nothing stellar, and throughout the year, he often called me to ask my opinion on various customer situations that he encountered. In each case, I told him my unvarnished opinion, and he began to listen. Later, in Tom's second year in business, sales started to really take off.

During one of my field visits to his store, as I was congratulating him, Tom smiled and said to me, "Jim, I have a confession to make."

"What do you mean, Tom?"

"As you know, I was not happy with my first year in business, and although I thought your methods about customer service were somewhat extreme, I decided to try it 'your' way."

"I see. Tell me more, Tom."

"Well, I'm not too big a man to admit it, but the 'Jim Palmer way' works!"

Tom then went on to share several stories about how his now-excited and dedicated customers were spending more and referring new customers to his business. It seems they were quite pleased with the way Tom always had their back.

It was one of the greatest franchise store visits I had, and a fantastic compliment that I've remembered to this day.

When thinking about the origin of what Tom called the "Jim Palmer way," I believe I first developed this mindset strategy during the severe recession that began in 1981. As our business began to shrink, we had fewer and fewer customers coming into the bike shop. I developed a two-pronged strategy to survive and prosper.

1) First, we had to maximize the profit potential of every customer we still had.

2) Second, I recognized the utter importance that each and every customer was to the survival of our business.

Every customer was critically important, and needed to be treated and valued as such. If we had an unhappy customer, my instincts were to swiftly react, based upon my deep concern of what would happen to this business if we ran out of customers.

When you view each and every customer situation as critical to the survival and success of your business, it instantly makes clear what the correct solution to the situation should be: Make them dazzled.

Whether a customer in our bike shop had a problem or complaint, or if I merely sensed that they weren't over-the-top happy with our products or service, I took swift action to correct the situation.

In my mind Losing a customer was simply not an option, and if they did leave, I did everything I could to ensure that they'd leave while still having a good feeling about our business.

This mindset strategy has been honed over my career, and is still very prevalent in my business today. Just ask my team.

As I was writing this book, I actually thought of naming it *The Jim Palmer Way*, but thought it would be confused with a book about baseball! So read on, enjoy the stories, and no matter what your business is, I urge you to try The Jim Palmer Way!

Acknowledgements

A Personal Thank You . . .

In many ways, this book is the culmination of a thirty-five year career in retail, franchise management, association management, and now as a business owner, speaker, and coach to other entrepreneurs. It sounds cliché, but this book truly could not have been written without the help of a great many people, including past employers, the many employees I've worked with, the thousands of customers I've interacted with, and the hundreds of authors, speakers, trainers, and mentors who have all helped to shape my views on both the proper mindset as well as the practical marketing and customer service strategies needed to sustain profitable growth.

I first want to thank the Lord for His love, patience, wisdom, and forgiveness. God has enriched and blessed my life in unimaginable ways.

I want to thank my wife, Stephanie, for being my best friend and just the perfect partner to share my life. As I write this note, we are days away from celebrating our 30th wedding anniversary in Hawaii. I can't imagine my life without her. I also want to thank Nick, Steve, Jessica, and Amanda, for being the absolute best children ever! Being your dad has meant more to me than anything, and you all give me so much to be proud of.

(L-R): Steve, Amanda, Stephanie, Nick, me, and Jessica, as we gathered for Christmas 2009.

While there are many mentors who have shaped my views on business, I especially want to thank Dan Kennedy and Bill Glazer for providing a business education that I feel certain is not available at any university. While my views on the importance of customer service and providing outstanding and memorable experiences have been formed over many years, the significant growth of my own businesses has occurred as a result of the entrepreneurial mindset and marketing strategies I've learned from Dan and Bill through my membership in Glazer-Kennedy Insider's Circle™ (www.DanKennedy.com).

I want to thank my amazing support team. Thank you to my amazing personal assistant, Kate; my Webmaster, Adam; my lead designer, Chris; Mike from Mikel Mailings, who handles the printing and mailing of my monthly No Hassle Newsletter program; Bobby from Synapse Print Management for being an outstanding partner for my Concierge Print and Mail On Demand program; my Newsletter Postcard production team, Sara, Roz, and Jennifer; and thank you to Ann Deiterich and Tammy Barley for doing a magnificent job editing this book.

Last, but certainly not least, I want to thank the countless customers and clients I've interacted with over the last thirty-five years. It is these individual experiences—the good, the bad, and the ugly—that have made me realize how vitally important over-the-top-happy customers are to a business. These customers are the lifeblood of any growing business, and it astounds me how many entrepreneurs and business owners fail to fully comprehend this fact. It is my sincere desire that this book will change some of these mindsets, enlighten some "stuck-in-the-mud" old-time thinking, and perhaps provide the entrepreneurial "let's-get-it-right" spark that so many businesses need, not just to survive but thrive, in this new economy.

To Your Success,

Jim Palmer

Chapter One: Getting 'Em or Keeping 'Em?

The Bonding Power of Glue

Whenever I think of glue, I remember the television commercial that showed a man holding on to his hard hat which was glued to a steel beam high in the air. Now that was strong glue! From a marketing perspective, it certainly was an attention-getting ad! In fact, based on this commercial, that was the glue that everyone wanted, so that they could fix what was broken!

What's the best glue you've ever used?

When I ask that question, I hear a lot of different brand names, but they all have one thing in common: they stick, they stick well, and they fix what's broken.

I'm certain your favorite glue shares those very same characteristics. That's exactly *why* it's your favorite, and the one you always reach for when things need fixing.

Imagine being able to get your customers to stick with you, just as well as if you used you favorite glue! That's what *Stick Like Glue* will help you to accomplish. If you adapt both the mindset and the successful business strategies that I describe in this book, I predict it will fix what is likely broken in your business.

I say that because I have never seen or heard of a business that isn't broken to some degree—some more than others—but for sure, all would be more profitable if their customers had more stick, and the stronger bonding power your glue has, the better!

The Leaky Bucket Analogy

When I speak around the country about newsletter marketing and effective customer retention strategies, I like to use the leaky bucket analogy.

Think of your company as a giant bucket of water. The water in your bucket represents your customers—the lifeblood of your business. Every drop of water that leaks out of your bucket is a lost customer and lost sales, including all future revenue. Ouch!

If your company is like a leaky bucket—and every business is to some degree—then it is paramount to your survival that you continuously fill your bucket with more water. After all, no water, no business!

So the question is: How leaky is your bucket? How many holes does your bucket have that are letting your customers constantly pour out?

Be honest—does your bucket simply have a few leaks around the seams that let customers occasionally seep out, or is it riddled it with holes, and customers are gushing out from every one of them?

If I can be blunt, my guess is that your bucket has more holes than you even know about. But don't be too embarrassed; most businesses do.

There are two ways to keep the water level in your bucket full and, therefore, customers in your business:

1) Constantly add more water, new customers, while previous customers continue to pour out.

2) Plug the leaks in your business, and keep the water you've already got in your bucket.

Getting 'Em

Most entrepreneurs spend a lot of *time, energy, and resources* on customer acquisition, and any entrepreneur will tell you that *time, energy, and resources* are the three most valuable commodities. They are also three of the most expensive and difficult marketing commodities to sustain.

I am an eager and continuous student of marketing and business. If you're like me, you've probably also read countless books and articles about different marketing strategies designed to help you get more new customers into your business.

With every passing week, and with the constant expansion of the Internet's power, it seems that there's always some new marketing strategy or tool to learn about, with each proclaiming to be the best way to get more customers. No doubt, it's a challenge to figure out what works best for attracting new customers to your business.

Marketing to Get New Customers Is Tough

Think about all the advertisements you see on any given day. If there's a space, there's an ad. Newspapers, magazines, billboards, the sides of buses, the roofs of taxicabs, hotel keys, and flip-down trays on airplanes all carry ads. There are even ads on the backs of bathroom stall doors.

Television and radio have long been supported by advertising, and you'll probably agree that the amount of broadcast advertising seems like it's surpassing actual programming content.

We're also exposed to a constant stream of messages vying for our attention online. Search ads, flash animation, pop-up boxes. With every click, there's another advertisement!

There's no escaping marketing messages.

Marketing to get new customers can be expensive and time-consuming. How can you compete? How can you get customers into your business?

Despite the rise of the Internet, direct mail advertising is still not only viable, it is incredibly effective. Just look in your mailbox if you don't agree. It's filled with postcards and letters enticing you to open them and read them. It must be working, or businesses wouldn't continue using this time-tested marketing method.

Unfortunately, direct mail advertising can be expensive and time-consuming. You've got to develop a campaign (or pay someone else to do it), design and print the ads (or pay someone else to do it), buy and/or maintain your list and mail it (or pay someone else to do it), and finally, measure the results (or pay someone else to do it).

As an entrepreneur or small business owner, how do you compete? How can you get more customers so you can increase your profits? Whatever marketing method or methods you use, it takes a lot of time, energy, and resources.

Maybe you've got sales representatives pounding the pavement and touting your products or services. If so, you know the expenses involved: commissions, benefits, mileage reports, quotas, training, and the list goes on.

Even if you opt for networking to spread the message about your company, you've still got to make a time investment, and, as an entrepreneur, you know that time really is money. How can you compete? How can you get customers?

Even if you've got the best marketing campaign in place and the most successful sales staff, you've got to track every effort to determine what's working and what's not. Failing to measure results is one of the quickest roads to business failure. How can you possibly know where to invest your efforts and resources without knowing what's working and what's not? If you're guessing, you might as well throw your hard-earned money into the wind and hope for the best.

There's no question about it—getting new customers has always been tough business, and in this current difficult economy, it's even more so! Getting 'em is very tough.

Is there a better way to grow your business?

I'm glad you asked. There is.

As an entrepreneur, you know just how difficult it can be to get new customers, so once you get them, you want to be sure to *keep* them…to be sure they "stick" around.

Keeping 'Em

It's far easier, and much more cost-effective, to keep the customers you have rather than trying to attract new ones. It's also much more profitable.

In other words, fix your leaky bucket rather than constantly add more water.

Selling more goods and services to customers you already know (and who know you) is far easier than constantly making first-time sales.

Think about it. Who would you rather call: a customer who you know will probably buy, or someone you've never met, to whom you'll have to explain your product or service *and* convince them it's got value *and* that you are a trustworthy and reputable business?

Ninety-nine entrepreneurs out of a hundred will pick the first choice. It's easier, and there's a greater likelihood for a positive outcome: a sale!

Your existing customers find value in what you offer, and they trust you. That's why they're your customers.

Building trust and rapport is the constant hurdle in cold-calling and prospecting. Nearly every new customer is distrusting at the beginning of a sales cycle.

Evaluate yourself as a consumer. When dealing with a new vendor, do you immediately trust the person/business? Probably not, unless they're a referral or have a long list of rock-solid testimonials. Even then, you may not trust them until you've verified the information for yourself. Your prospects are no different. Why should they be?

Sticky Note:
According to Zig Ziglar, every sale has five basic obstacles: no need, no money, no hurry, no desire, and...
NO TRUST!

The first four of those obstacles are difficult enough to overcome. Why burden your efforts by having to clear the *trust* hurdle as well? With your existing customers, you don't have to. You've already established trust and rapport.

With all that said, let me be perfectly clear: I'm not suggesting that you forego or turn off your new customer acquisition marketing efforts. Not at all! To the contrary, every business, large and small, must always have its marketing funnel wide open to attract and catch as many new customers as possible. However, I believe that too many businesses focus every last marketing dollar on customer acquisition, and, to their detriment, they spend little or nothing on building, maintaining, and strengthening the relationships they already have with their current customers. This is a mistake.

When you think about, it's really backwards. Remember the 80/20 rule: 80 percent of your profits come from 20 percent of your customers. Too many companies spend 100 percent of their marketing budget on new customer acquisition, instead of where it has the greatest chance of yielding the largest return on investment: current customers. Does doing that make sense? Of course not! Instead, dedicate the proper percentage of your marketing budget and efforts to the place where it has already proven to produce results—your current customers.

No matter what business you're in, your greatest source of new revenue is with your existing customers. Plus, the longer they are customers, the more likely they are to spend more with you and refer new customers. Take advantage of that! Plug the holes in your bucket!

(Sorry, guys, but duct tape won't get *this* job done. You'll need *glue*.)

Sticky Note:
According to Frederick Reichheld, fellow at Bain & Company, a prestigious management and consulting firm, and author of *Loyalty Rules*, it costs five times more to obtain new clients than it does to retain and resell to existing ones.

You're Sitting on a Gold Mine

You may not realize it, but you're sitting on a gold mine. Simply look at your current customer list. "There's gold in them thar names!"

There are really only two ways to grow your business:

1) Get more clients, or
2) Sell more to those you already have.

Profitable, growing businesses are the ones that are plugging the holes in their leaky buckets and keeping their existing clients longer. Getting your current customers to stick to you like glue is the key to your organization's growth and long-term profitability.

In fact, for every 1 percent increase you achieve in customer retention, there's a 7 percent increase in profitability. That's huge! (That's also according to Bain & Company.)

So with that in mind, and knowing that it's five times more costly to acquire new customers than to grow the ones you already have, you've got to have some really great glue, so keep reading.

Sticking Points:

Here's the recap of the important points to remember about acquisition (getting 'em) versus retention (keeping 'em):

- View each and every customer situation as critical to the survival and success of your business.

- It's easier and more cost-effective to plug the holes in your leaky bucket than it is to constantly add water.

- You can't ignore acquiring new customers, but dedicate the right proportion of your marketing budget to retention.

- Remember the 80/20 Rule: 80% of your profits come from 20% of your customers!

- There are only two ways to grow your business: get more customers *or* sell more to the ones you already have.

- The longer they are your customers, the more likely they are to spend more with you and refer new customers.

- Remember that a 1% increase in customer retention generates a 7% increase in profits!

- It's five times more costly to acquire new customers than to grow the ones you already have.

Chapter Two:
Increasing Adhesion

Strategies to Develop and Build Stronger Customer Relationships

Have you ever tried to glue something, only to find that the glue was actually stronger than what you applied it to, so the end result was another break?

The same thing can happen when trying to stick like glue to your customers. If your foundation isn't very strong, the best glue in the world won't help you.

Your foundation is the relationship you have with your customers. It is your level of *customer service*—the way your business treats and values customers.

In order to succeed in any business, excellent customer service is paramount. I've always stood on the principle that you can never go too far with customer service.

Bill Glazer, internationally recognized marketing expert and president of Glazer Kennedy Insider's Circle™, uses the phrase, "Inspect what you expect." By that, he means that you should honestly evaluate how your company is addressing your customers.

How? There are two excellent ways.

1) You can pose as a customer, or
2) You can have someone play that role on your behalf—this is known as mystery shopping (you'll learn more about this in the bonus chapter!).

"Inspect What You Expect"

Whichever way you choose to evaluate your company as a customer, you should evaluate by using the following criteria, just as your customers do:

Telephone

- What's your impression of when and how you're greeted on the phone?
- Is the person pleasant to speak with?
- If you have an automated system, is your options menu easy to navigate?
- If you have an automated system, is it easy to connect with a real live person?
- Is your outgoing voice-mail message professional and friendly?
- Is your outgoing voice-mail message current?

      How many times have you called somebody and heard an outgoing message that was from a just-past holiday, or perhaps from their vacation two months ago? Don't laugh. Something that simple sends the wrong message to your customers.

Web site

- Is your URL simple and easy to remember?
- Is your Web site easy to find online?
- Do your Web pages load quickly?
- Are your color choices reflective of your store and customer base?
- Are your color choices welcoming and compelling?
- Are your color choices intriguing, yet comfortable on the eyes?
- Are your graphics reflective of your store and customer base?

- Do your graphics add visual interest, or do they overwhelm the customer? (Keep in mind that too many graphics can make your Web pages slow to load.)
- Are your font choices, and sizes, easy to read so that customers can easily find what they want?
- Is your Web site easy to navigate, or is it a cluttered mess filled with way too many options?
- If you have a brick-and-mortar store, does your Web site provide a map for finding your store?
- Does your Web site list store hours?
- Does it provide a telephone number so that customers can call for more information (and speak with a real live person)?
- Is your online store easy to use?
- Does your online store answer questions about shipping and delivery dates?
- What's the first thing visitors see when they go to your Web site? Does this make them want to stay at your Web site?

Store

If you've got a brick and mortar shop, what's the first thing customers notice when they walk through your door, or even before that…

- Does your outdoor signing make it easy for first-time customers to find your store from the road?
- When they park their cars, is the parking lot clean and orderly?
- Is the parking lot smoothly paved or blacktopped, with striping that is easy to see? (Got potholes? Fill them!)
- What about your parking lot signs, are they worn and looking like they should have been replaced a year ago?
- Is your parking lot aesthetically pleasing?
- Do trees provide cooling shade on hot summer days?

- Is the landscaping well-maintained and free of weeds?
- Is your parking lot lit well at night?
- Are there signs in your window promoting an event that took place five months ago?
- Are your windows clean?
- Inside the store, how quickly are you greeted, or at least acknowledged, in person?
- Is the store clean (especially the bathrooms!)?

I remember management guru, Tom Peters, saying one time that coffee stains on the flip-down trays mean that the airline doesn't care about engine maintenance. Fair or not, your customers form opinions from their initial contact with your company.

Once, when I was a regional manager for a chain of stores, I visited one of the stores I was responsible for, and the first two things I noticed were greasy handprints all over the door and that the carpet was filthy. When I questioned the manager, he said he and the store were busy and the vacuum cleaner was broken. I told him that while both of these reasons (excuses) could be true, the customers who came to this store didn't know how busy he was or that his vacuum cleaner was broken, and, fair or not, they would draw the conclusion that this business didn't care about quality. Cleanliness matters!

- Is this store a place where you feel comfortable and enjoy being?
- Do you have a store layout map or signing that allows customers to find what they're looking for easily?
- Are sales associates easy to find, either by their clothing or by name tags?
- Are your questions answered promptly and courteously?
- Are you assisted thoroughly, promptly, and courteously?
- Did you find it easy to do business with your company?

- Did you leave with a smile on your face?

The reality is, if your customers are not smiling when they leave your store, and saying to themselves, "Wow, that was a great experience," it's not likely that they'll be sharing this experience with others.

The sad truth is that today customer service is at an all-time low. It seems that most companies prefer to put their customers in an incredibly difficult-to-navigate maze of voice mail rather than talk to them. Automated systems are cost-effective, but we all complain about voice-mail hell. The Internet offers a wealth of benefits to conducting business 24/7/365, but it means a lot of self-service, and many sites are difficult to navigate. If you visit most stores, you're greeted by someone who has no customer training whatsoever, if you're greeted at all. And when's the last time you needed to ask a question or get help in one of the mega chain "big box" stores? How'd you make out? Could you even find anyone to help you? Even the storewide announcement "Special assistance needed in aisle seven; special assistance needed in aisle seven" rarely brings prompt, special assistance.

That's the bad news. The good news is that since customer service is at such an all-time low, it's really easy to stand out and be recognized– and talked about—as a great place to do business with.

It's my belief that if you simply make it easy for someone to do business with you, and if you are polite and courteous, you will have happy customers. If you go just a few extra steps to make your customers' experiences with you memorable, they will be singing your praises from the rooftops!

If you can't honestly assess the above telephone, Web site, and store criteria, ask someone, such as a secret shopper, to do it for you. *Then act on any negative reports immediately.*

When you "inspect what you expect" then plug those leaks, you are on your way to "keeping 'em," with a solid strategy to develop and build stronger customer relationships: You are meeting and exceeding your customer expectations.

That is awesome glue!

The Ivory Tower

Over the years, I've found that "inspect what you expect" thinking often falls short, especially in large corporations, as you move from the front lines of customer service toward what I call the "Ivory Tower." The Ivory Tower is where policies and procedures are enacted by folks who rarely, if ever, spend time interacting with customers. The result—those policies are often silly, and sometimes ridiculous, when implemented on the front lines.

If only those upper-management folks sitting in the Ivory Towers would "inspect what they expected," they'd quickly see how the very policies and procedures they create often interfere with their ability to meet and exceed customer expectations, and, thus, interfere with their ability to grow their business.

Twenty-five years in retail has ingrained in me an ability to spot such stupidity a mile away, as I did recently, so let me share the story to illustrate this point.

I was on a tight schedule, as usual, and one of my stops was at my personal bank to deposit a check. I pulled into the drive-through, and, after waiting almost twelve minutes (while still on that tight schedule), the teller returned to tell me that he couldn't deposit my check because it appeared altered.

What?

It was my own company check, written by me, to myself, to be deposited (not cashed!) into my personal checking account that I had with this bank!

It seems that the bank has a policy of not accepting checks that may appear to be altered. At first glance, this seems like a worthwhile safety policy for all concerned, so I asked what the specific objection was.

The teller explained that the date looked altered. He said that he couldn't tell if the date was February 12 or 13. It was not altered, perhaps my messy handwriting made it look that way, but in either case, what difference could this possibly make? It was February 13th! At this point, I really wasn't mad, I was stunned in disbelief.

I realized that the teller was simply following bank procedure (dictated by someone in the Ivory Tower) and that the teller was not the one to be upset with. So I asked if the manager was inside. He said that she was, but that she already okayed this! "Tell her I'll be right in."

I drove around, parked, and went inside where the manager was waiting for me. She re-explained the bank's policy, and showed me that the date on my check was not clear. Since it was already February 13th, I asked what possible difference it could make, and she simply repeated the bank's "no-alterations" policy. I would need to bring back another check.

Now I was getting steamed.

Here are the facts of this situation as I explained them to the branch manager, who, by the way, knows me by sight!

- You recognize and know me by sight as one of your customers.
- You personally opened up our checking and savings accounts.
- You processed our home equity loan six months ago.
- You know that I own my own business, and that this is my company check, written by me.
- And finally, I'm not looking to withdraw money; I'm trying to deposit this money into your bank!

No dice. She told me that I had to write another check and come back.

Despite my utter disbelief and, I believe, red face, I still recognized that even the branch manager was not the policy maker, so I asked who was, and if we could get that person on the phone!

Surprisingly, she obliged. She got the bank's corporate Ivory-Tower controller on the phone to further clarify the bank's no-alterations policy. The branch manager told the controller the facts as I just outlined above, and then asked the Ivory-Tower controller, "Even though I know Jim, if I accept this check, someone in Compliance will write me up, right?" She was told, "Yes, they will."

And there you have it. The branch manager, who appeared to have an ounce of common sense, and was trying her best to help me, her customer, was simply afraid for her job. The result was one of major inconvenience for a good customer. Not good.

By the way, this bank has also been courting me for six months to move my business banking to their bank. Not going to happen.

This is an example of a policy created in the Ivory Tower, combined with zero tolerance for any common sense to be applied by the very folks entrusted to interact with and serve their customers.

Many times, company policies are created in the heat of the moment, when something bad or unfortunate happens at the store level. Typically, the policies created are an overreaction to something that rarely happens and, in fact, create impediments to the very customers with whom they are trying to do business.

Do you have any of these Ivory-Tower policies in your business?

Do you trust your frontline staff to do what's necessary to serve and please your customers?

And, more importantly, does you staff know that you "have their back" and will not come down on them for trying to please a customer?

Remember, customers have many options other than your business. Make it *easy* for your customers to do business with you!

By the way, when I left the bank, I drove to another branch location less than two miles away. They immediately deposited my check. So much for consistency!

I believe that the vast majority, perhaps 98 percent, of customers are honest and not out to take advantage of a business. Unfortunately, when a customer does take advantage of a situation or does something completely dishonest, too many companies overreact and create policies that adversely affect the vast majority of honest customers.

So really evaluate your policies. If you have some that were put in place as knee-jerk reactions, they probably only address about 2 percent of your customer base, and create roadblocks for the 98 percent who are trying to do business with you.

The choice is yours. You *can* dig your heels in and determine that it's your way or no way, but at the end of the day, you bank deposit is going to be smaller.

There you have it—a second strategy to develop and build stronger customer relationships so that you increase adhesion: Evaluate your Ivory-Tower policies.

Sticky Note:

In my retail days, when I was training store employees or new franchise owners, as we had this discussion of customer service, I would tell them that it's okay if you choose to be right—but most of the time your bank deposit will be smaller as a result. For me, I learned to be okay with siding with the customer, even if they were wrong, because it usually meant that my bank deposit would be larger!

Easy Does It

Make it *easy* for your customers to do business with you. This concept is so important to developing and building stronger customer relationships that I'm going to focus just on that for a moment.

As a customer, have you ever walked into a place and heard the phrase "That's our policy?" Those words are like a slap in the face with a cold, dead fish. I'm certain you don't like hearing it, and I certainly didn't appreciate that approach to my seemingly altered check at the bank. Well, neither do your customers! Even if you fill a very unique niche with your product or service, if you stand on policy or your terms and conditions at every turn, customers will figure out how to get what they need from someone else.

My dental office has a sign posted right on the reception desk about their rules and policies. Is that really what I want to see as soon as I walk into the office? Of course not. No one does. You immediately send a bad message to your customers with that type of signage. In effect, you're saying "Here are all the hoops you have to jump through and all the bridges you have to cross before we'll take your money." It's a cardinal sin to make it difficult for customers to hand you money!

Here's another example from my bike days regarding the impact of Ivory-Tower policy-making that made it difficult to do business with us and created roadblocks for customers *who were there to give us money*:

With most bike purchases, customers want to take test rides beforehand. At one point, we had a bike stolen during a test ride, and I had to report that to headquarters. The next thing you know, there's a meeting at the corporate level about instituting policies to curb theft, and the retail locations began receiving rules and terms and conditions that were to be mounted next to the register. The policy was that, in order to take a test ride, customers had to leave a credit card or driver's license. I did not like having to hang this up, because I saw this as an overreaction to a rare situation and believed it would become an impediment to doing business.

Since I believe that 98 percent of people are honest, I do not want to create policies, procedures, terms, and conditions to combat the 2 percent who seek to take advantage of me. Creating policies and procedures to combat the dishonest 2 percent makes it more difficult and a less-pleasant experience for the 98 percent of honest people to give you money—also known as profit! Sure, we need to be smart business owners, but I strongly encourage you to not overreact to the occasional negative situation. Instead, stay focused on the larger picture.

Make certain you are easy to do business with.

Be Accessible

Another way to develop and build stronger customer relationships is also one of the foundations of great service: Be accessible to your customers.

Really serve them. It's why you're in business and the only way to grow and be profitable. Whatever you do to create happy customers pays off!

What can you do? Return calls, answer e-mails, and address complaints, *promptly*. I know it may sound strange, but, over time, I grew to look forward to the occasional problem or upset customer because I became so skilled at diffusing the situation and ultimately creating a raving fan! (Lots more about addressing complaints in a later chapter!)

If at all possible, your customers should not be forced to your voice mail or your Web site as the only means of contacting you. That does absolutely nothing to build trust. Embrace people over technology whenever possible. Your customers will relate to you and your employees. They will not necessarily relate to your automated systems.

Certainly, voice mail, e-mail, and auto-responders have their place, and I use them in my business, but that should not be your only contact with your customers. I have a team of support people who know I expect all customer inquiries and problems to be addressed quickly, certainly within twenty-four hours if at all possible.

A little effort toward simply being accessible goes a long way toward increasing customer adhesion.

Pain Points

No matter how much your customers like you, they're really buying the solutions you offer, and they're buying to eliminate their pain points. Remember that your product or service must be of some benefit to them and make their lives easier and/or more enjoyable and potentially relieve some of their pain. After all, every single one of us has the same favorite radio station: WII-FM (What's In It for Me?).

For an auto repair shop, the customers' pain point is often the inconvenience of getting their cars serviced. They have to drop off the car, and then find a ride to get home or to work. If there was a trustworthy mechanic who offered this service, it would be exactly the solution most customers needed, and it would ease their pain point. Now, if that same auto shop washed and vacuumed the car in addition to servicing it, that would be over-the-top customer service—and certainly worthy of much word-of-mouth advertising!

I'll also give you a marketing example, since most successful businesses address pain points in their marketing efforts. I know I do.

In my newsletter business, I know there are two recurring pain points that customers have regarding establishing a successful monthly newsletter marketing program: "It takes too long to write and produce a newsletter," and "I never know what to include as content that my customers will read and enjoy." It's no coincidence that those are exactly the benefits of No Hassle

Newsletters, and my marketing addresses these pain points in a big way.

When thinking about your marketing, envision your most perfect target customer, and address your message specifically to that person, keeping in mind his or her pain points. Don't envision addressing a stadium full of people. Imagine the one person who is your perfect customer.

For me, my perfect customer is "John." John is a thirty-eight-year-old entrepreneur and small business owner. Like many other small business entrepreneurs, John has heard that customer newsletters are good for business, and John may have even occasionally tried one. John's pain is that he has a lot of other duties and responsibilities on his plate, and has trouble carving out time to write and produce a monthly newsletter. I address his pain and offer my famous Customer-Loving™ Content, and ready-to-go newsletter templates, and I offer the ability to produce a kick-butt monthly newsletter that will get results in less than 23 minutes per month! Problem solved; pain alleviated; happy customer!

Trust me on this. I have hundreds of happy clients in seven countries. Cure your customers' pains, and you'll be on your way to having customers that stick, and having a profitable business.

Sticky Note:
Always imagine your perfect customer and know what the pain point is...what keeps him up at night. Successful marketing addresses alleviating this pain.

Keeping pain points in mind works in marketing, and also while you're being accessible to your customers, whether in person or via telephone or Web site.

Keep your eyes and ears open when communicating with your existing customers for their pain points. Sometimes they'll raise a red flag immediately, and your response and remedy should be immediate as well.

The other morning, I had a message from a brand-new client saying that he had difficulty logging into the membership area of our Web site. I immediately followed up and responded, and also had my support team check out the site for any possible errors. Turns out there was not a problem—he was not using his correct username and password—but our swift attention to his problem not only made him very happy, it also helped to pave the way for a longer relationship, because the trust factor was enhanced.

Keeping customers means alleviating their pain and agony, and also addressing any suspicions they may have about their purchase—another potential pain point. If our Web site doesn't work properly, a new customer may be suspicious that he or she might have been scammed, or perhaps feel that they bought into a substandard program. That is precisely why my team and I react so quickly.

Prompt follow-up and problem resolution are important for all businesses, but it's especially true for Internet-based operations. Letting your online customers know that there are real people running the show, that there are real people looking out for their best interest, is a great way to build their trust and loyalty.

Address whatever pain points arise with your existing customers immediately, so they'll continue to do business with you. It's just good, solid customer service, and makes for good customer adhesion.

In addition to two-way communication with your customers, listen for *recurring* problems. Those recurrences are indicators that you're not easy to do business with in some way, shape, or form, and you'll want to fix that in order to keep your customers glued.

Back in my bike-business days, I realized that our operating hours were not conducive to serving our customers. While our hours were typical for many specialty retail stores in the early '80s (no evening hours and closed Mondays), after hearing similar complaints about our accessibility, specifically in the after-work evening hours, I began to keep the store open two nights each week until 9:00 p.m. We also began opening the store on Mondays, which I have to tell you, was not a popular move with my staff or my competitors. But the results were amazing!

Anything your customer tells you that makes it difficult for him or her to do business with you is a pain point. Fix it. Don't ever view that sort of feedback simply as a complaint. Your customer is signaling you that he or she would like to continue doing business but is encountering some roadblocks.

The other reason that you should welcome this type of customer feedback is that, in many cases, it is often easier for customers to simply walk away and avoid confrontation. Fix your customers' pain points! Be easy to do business with! Your customers' only job is to get out their credit cards or write checks. Your job is to do everything else. You're in business to serve your customers.

Sticky Note:
WI-WI-WI: What I Want—When I Want It—Where I Want It. Profitable and growing businesses understand that they must address and cater to their customers' WI-WI-WI desires.

Under-Promise and Over-Deliver

One of the easiest ways to increase customer adhesion is to manage their expectations. Managing their expectations is a matter of under-promising and over-delivering.

No doubt you've experienced this as a consumer. I know I have. I buy from the same computer company all the time, and with every order, I'm told my new computer will arrive in 10 to 14 days. Without fail, every one of my orders has arrived in 5 to 7 days—half the time that I was told. I'm thrilled! I think, "Wow, what great service. It's faster than I thought." My expectations have been managed. They under-promised and over-delivered.

The same thing happens at some restaurants…well, at the successful ones anyway. You're told the wait will be 30 minutes, and you're seated in 15 minutes. You're very pleased. Your expectations have been managed.

As we've said, since poor customer service seems to be rampant in this day and age, it's pretty easy to make customers happy.

In my wildly popular business, No Hassle Newsletters (www.NoHassleNewsletters.com), in addition to providing clients with my famous "Customer-Loving™ Content" and ready-to-use-newsletter templates, I also create custom mastheads for my clients who want to personalize their company newsletters. Customers are told that it will take 10 days to have the finished product to them and ready to use. Then we work very hard to get it to them in 5 to 7 days. Additionally, when prospects are learning about No Hassle Newsletters at my Web site, I tell them that in many cases it will take 6 to 9 months to see some positive results in their businesses from their monthly customer newsletter. But plenty of people see results sooner than that. If it happens sooner, I've managed their expectations. I've beaten what I've told them to expect and created a raving fan of newsletter marketing in general, and No Hassle Newsletters in particular.

One last example from my business: When a client e-mails us for support, the Web site sends an automatic reply e-mail letting them know that they can expect a reply within 24 hours. In most cases, my support staff replies within a few hours, if not sooner. Does this help to build trust and value, and build stronger customer relationships? You bet it does.

Sticky Note:

If you don't believe this to be true, I suggest you try the opposite. Tell a customer you'll have his order ready in two days, and then deliver it in five!

Sticking Points:

Here's the recap of the important points to remember about developing and building strong customer relationships:

 You can never go too far with customer service.

 "Inspect what you expect." Test how your organization treats your customers and their impressions of your business.

 Be easy to do business with. Get rid of any policies that create impediments to the majority of customers who want to do business with you.

 Ninety-eight percent of your customers are not going to take advantage of you. They want to give you money.

 Excise the phrase "That's company policy" (or any reference to terms and conditions) from your vocabulary.

 Be accessible to your customers. Address complaints immediately and to the satisfaction of your customer.

 Keep your eyes and ears open to find out your customers' pain points. Address them immediately.

 Listen for recurring problems. Address them immediately.

 Manage expectations: Under-promise and over-deliver to create happy customers.

Chapter Three:
What's It Really Worth?

Calculating Your Customers' Lifetime Value

You may still be wondering why customer retention is so important. I can answer that in two words: Lifetime Value.

As we saw with the 80/20 rule, existing customers provide the bulk of your profits. It's more cost-effective to sell to existing customers, so your profitability is higher.

However, the profitability of existing customers goes far beyond their current sales figures, and that's what lifetime value (LTV) is all about.

Before we get to the math and explanations of calculating LTV, I want to share two stories with you that demonstrate how over-the-top customer service and LTV fit together, and how they directly affect your bottom line.

When I was in the bike business, a man came into the store one day, carrying an obviously bent front wheel from his kid's bike. Viewed from the side, the wheel's shape was round…round…round…until you got to one section that was shaped exactly like a street curb.

The guy was visibly angry, because he'd probably spent $300 for the bike, and, other than the mangled shape, the wheel looked shiny-new.

So he's carrying it in, and proceeds to tell me the wheel is "defective." My mechanics were watching, and wondering how I'd handle this one.

I asked the man if he knew how it happened. He said, "My kid was out riding his new bike, and this is the result." I had to give him some credit for not lying while trying to pull one over on me.

I told him that I understood he was upset, and that I would also be upset having spent so much for the bike only to have this happen. I then took the wheel and asked him to come outside with me, and I placed the damaged part of the wheel right against the curb in our parking lot. It was a perfect fit, and he realized immediately that his kid must have ridden his brand-new $300 bike into a curb.

I said, "Look, I know you spent a lot of money on the bike just a week ago. Here's what I'd like to do for you." (*For you* being key words in the conversation.) "Let's get the bike out of your car, and let me install a brand-new wheel."

The customer appeared somewhat flabbergasted. He asked me what the cost would be. I said, "Nothing. We'll cover this one for you, and you can explain to your son how bike wheels and curbs are generally not a good match."

Having performed such over-the-top acts of customer service many times before, I already knew the predictable next step—this guy's whole demeanor instantly changed. He smiled and appeared to become my best friend! Despite the irrefutable proof that his kid messed up, my store was going to cover him. He told me that he really appreciated my offer and would not forget it.

The retail cost of a new wheel is $60, and labor would have been $15. We could have made $75 on the deal. While we didn't create the problem or deserve to replace the wheel for free, in his initial mindset when he angrily walked in the door, the overall bike-buying experience with our store had not been great. It was tainted. I went over the top, to make him not just satisfied, but happy.

This customer went on to purchase a bike for himself, his wife, and his daughter over the next few months. If it were you, where else would you buy your bikes? Plus, where do you think he told his friends and neighbors to shop when they were looking for bikes?

Here's the bottom line, in my opinion: While the mechanics accused me of giving away the shop (the wheel obviously wasn't defective), we weren't out that much. The $60 wheel cost us about $30, and my mechanic was already on the clock, so the labor didn't cost me an extra dollar. So for a $30 investment (hey, I can't buy a TV ad, radio ad, and can't do much of a mailing for $30), I'm way ahead of the game.

This type of over-the-top service almost always reaps huge dividends, and, as I said in this case, I sold at least three more bikes as a result of this customer service strategy.

I've shared this story often while training employees, but one day, when I was relating this story to a new franchise owner whom I was training, he said, "Jim, I can see your point, but there's got to be a limit to this type of over-the-top strategy. After all, you can't give away the business." So I shared an even more outrageous, over-the-top customer service story and the results:

I once worked for a company that sold slate billiard tables which ranged in price from $1000 to $5000. After we sold a table and installed it, customers had the option to call us back within sixty days to return and re-level it. Due to the table's weight, it was pretty typical for a pool table to need re-leveling, especially if the table was installed on carpet.

Well, we sold and installed a $1500 table, and then went out and re-leveled it once…twice…three times. It really wasn't out of level, but the customer thought that for the amount he paid (in his mind, a lot of money), he wanted it to be absolutely perfect. Ultimately, we went back out five times, and after the fifth time, he called back and claimed the table was defective. While he appreciated our policy to re-level tables, he questioned how many times we were going to have to re-level it. In his mind, the table was defective, and he demanded another one. Yikes!

The installation for a pool table typically took about four hours, and I paid a team about $300 to do it. On top of that, I knew I'd be stuck with a used table if I gave in to his demand. But I swallowed hard and said, "I want you to be happy, so I'm going to give you a new table." He was, obviously, very happy with my offer. After installing his new table, which, by the way, he paid more for an upgraded table (perhaps his original reason for asking for a new one), we then set his original one up on the sales floor and, after using it as a demo, sold it at a discount.

What was the result? I know for a fact that we sold two more pool tables that season to his friends. When they came into our store, they said that they didn't know what they wanted, but they told us that they wanted to buy one from us. "Joe says you guys are the best, so I want to buy it here."

My total investment was another $300 to install the second table, and I discounted the used table as a demo model and sold it for $1200, so I was really out about $500 total, but I sold two more tables, and our reputation was one of providing huge, over-the-top customer service.

I never asked Joe for the referrals, but this was such an over-the-top and unbelievable experience for him, that he kept referring us. You can't buy that type of marketing results for $500, and it all contributes to the customer's LTV.

Sticky Note:
Don't be shortsighted or cheap when it comes to satisfying your customers. You can be right or you can have a bigger bank deposit. You really do reap what you sow.

So, the bottom line is this: In my opinion, it's nearly impossible to give away the business trying to do what's best for your customer, because the dividends paid on your efforts always outweigh the investment.

By the Book

BusinessDictionary.com defines Lifetime Value as, "Total profit (or loss) estimated to result from an ongoing business relationship with a customer over the life of relationship. Goods or services with high lifetime value may justify comparatively higher marketing expenditure and/or salesperson compensation. Also called lifetime proceeds."

The most important thing to remember about LTV is that every customer represents the potential for cumulative sales. When you lose a customer, you lose not just that sale but every future sale as well.

If I would have insisted that the bike wheel wasn't defective and charged the man to replace it, I still would have had the initial sale of $300 on my books plus the $75 replacement, but because of the over-the-top customer service I gave him instead, his LTV turned into much, much more.

The same thing is true in the case of the billiard table owner. His original sale was $1500, and if we would not have replaced his table to keep him happy, his LTV would have probably also been $1500. Because we went over the top, he made three referrals and turned his LTV into about $5000 to $6000.

LTV calculations are built on your customers' histories. In its very simplest form, LTV is your customers' average sales multiplied by the average number of times they reorder.

As I said, that's the very simplest calculation, because LTV calculations actually project into the future, so you should take it farther in order to understand how it can impact your opportunity to grow your business.

It's important to know how long customers stay with you, in addition to knowing how many times they reorder and the average value of each order.

Sticky Note:
Lifetime Value =
Average Sale x Average # of reorders x Length of Time

Once you establish the LTV, you can use it as the benchmark for developing a realistic customer acquisition and *retention* budget.

It's worthwhile to carefully review your records, to get the most accurate estimates of these numbers, before you attempt any calculations. As they say, junk in, junk out. You want to be certain you're basing your decisions on the most accurate data. Let's look at an example.

Variable	Value	Calculation
Number of Customers:	60	Based on the time period for which you're calculating the LTV.
Number of Sales:	100	This represents the number of orders you've filled, not the number of products sold.
Total Value of All Sales:	$15,000	This is based on your records for the specified period.
Average Value of a Sale:	$150	Divide the total value of sales by the number of sales. In this case: $15,000 / 100.
Number of times the average customer reorders:	1.666	Divide the number of sales you've made by the number of customers you have.
Average LTV:	$249.90	Multiply the average value by the average number of reorders. In this case: $150 x 1.666.

This is the simplest calculation, but it does not take into account the value of retention, and retention is your greatest opportunity for profitability and growth.

The goal is to extend the length of time each customer remains as your customer, so you can really leverage their LTV. In the simple calculation above, you can easily double, triple, or quadruple that answer by retaining the customer. Here are two important facts about LTV and retention:

- The retention rate increases with every passing year. (In other words, the longer customers stay with you, the longer they tend to stay.)
- Both the number of customer orders, and the value of each order, tend to increase.

So, what's over-the-top customer service really worth? I'll answer that in this way: There are only three ways to grow your revenue:

1) Get new customers.
2) Increase the number of times existing customers order from you.
3) Increase the value of each order.

As we've already seen, it's easier and much more cost-effective to keep customers than it is to get new ones. When you keep them, they're going to order more often, and increase what they spend on each order. Besides sticking with you longer and spending more, the cost of selling to retained customers decreases. Since they already know you and trust you, they're much quicker to make another purchase, shortening the sales cycle and reducing your marketing efforts. When costs go down, your profitability goes up! Now you can really get things moving, because increased profitability means you can increase the discounts you offer to your most loyal customers which, in turn, promotes even more buying activity and even more loyalty.

The heart and soul of ongoing—and increased—profits is retention. *Glue.* The longer and stronger your customers stick, the more they spend.

And the bottom line in getting them to stick is to make them happy—to meet and exceed their expectations.

If you don't have happy customers, if your company is not the first one that pops into their minds when they need what you sell, then you don't have a profitable business, or one that's growing to the magnitude it should be. When you've got raving fans, your company will not only be the first one that pops into their minds, it will be the only one. They won't even think of shopping elsewhere.

Let me share one more short story to help make this point.

My franchise attorney once gave me this advice: "Jim, after a franchisee signs the contract, your goal is to put it in the file drawer and hope you never have to look at it again."

"Huh?"

"Jim," he said, "it's simple. You do whatever it takes to keep your franchisees happy, because prospective franchisees are going to ask current franchise owners about their experience with your company. And if you're not treating them well, or if they *perceive* that they're not being treated fairly, they're going to mention that to everyone they can. If you're only doing what you need to do contractually, as described by the words in the franchise agreement, that is clearly not the best way to grow."

So, if you have to think about whether or not investing in customer relationships, and going out of your way to serve your customers, is worthwhile, if you're only doing what you're "contractually obligated" to do, you're not going to be profitable and grow. You're really undercutting yourself!

What's it really worth? If you want to strengthen and grow your business, then it's worth applying some over-the-top-customer-service glue to make your customers stick!

Sticking Points:

Here's the recap of the important points to remember about LTV:

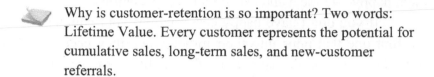

- Why is customer-retention is so important? Two words: Lifetime Value. Every customer represents the potential for cumulative sales, long-term sales, and new-customer referrals.

- Retained customers are more profitable. It costs less to sell to them, so they really impact your bottom line.

- Over-the-top customer service almost NEVER fails to pay off, and it improves your customers' LTVs.

- When you lose a customer, you don't just lose a sale—you lose his entire LTV—all his future sales *and* his referrals.

- Simple Calculation:
  LTV = Average Sale x Average # of reorders x Length of Time

- Improving retention rates dramatically improves LTV.

- A customer's order quantities and values increase proportionately with retention.

- Retention rates increase year after year. The longer you've got a customer, the longer you tend to keep him.

- Repeat business doesn't simply "speak" volumes about your company; it screams them.

Chapter Four:
The Best Glue Ever

Customer Service Strategies That Increase Your Stick!

You've probably heard it said that charity begins at home. You might be surprised to learn that charity in your workplace improves your glue and increases the likelihood of customers sticking with you for life.

How do you treat your employees? If you're of the mindset that you pay them and they should do exactly whatever you demand, whenever you demand it, period (after all, you're the boss, right?), chances are your business is probably not growing as well as it should. Attitudes trickle down, both good and bad.

To put it simply, if you treat your employees well, they're going to treat your customers well. When your customers are treated well, they're going to stick around.

Treating employees well doesn't always mean paying them top-dollar salaries, although that helps a great deal. Study after study on employee satisfaction indicates that money is not a leading motivator. *Being recognized for their efforts* and *having empowerment* often lead the list.

Reward employees whenever you catch them doing something right. That's one the easiest and most meaningful forms of recognition.

That said, since recognition and other effective strategies on employee motivation can easily fill its own book, let's focus on empowerment, because that has a huge and immediate impact on your level of customer service.

Empowerment

Let your employees know, and make it crystal clear, that you want them to do whatever it takes to make your customers happy, so that customers become raving fans. If this book had only room for one sentence, it would be this:

Happy customers who become raving fans are the surest way to a successful, profitable business.

Yet, too often, I see business owners worry about their employees "giving away the shop" when they give their employees empowerment. This is simply a worry that never materializes. How much would they really have to give away to go negative against your customers' lifetime values? You simply *can't* give away the shop.

If you give away just barely enough to make customers happy, are they going to stick with you for life, refer others to you, and become raving fans? Probably not. They may come back periodically because it wasn't a negative experience, but experience tells us that raving fans are created by over-the-top service. Be certain your employees know that they have your blessing to do whatever it takes to send your customers away over-the-top happy.

Sticky Note:
"Our only rule: Use good judgment in all situations."
—Excerpt from the Nordstrom Employee Handbook, Nordstrom, Inc., Seattle, WA

I believe it is paramount that you instill in your employees the attitude that serving the customer is really what drives their paychecks, for this simple reason: It is. Too many employees focus on completing their tasks and/or daily responsibilities and wrongly see customers as distractions to their day.

This is not to say it's all the employee's fault. In many cases, this attitude permeates from the top.

I have always done best when I hire for attitude and train the skills, rather than hiring someone with a lot of industry experience and a bad attitude.

Obviously, from what you've read so far, you know that I've always been a huge proponent for providing the best customer service. A major part of this strategy is that I've always let my employees know that I want them to do whatever it takes to make customers happy. If I think an employee's approach could have been handled a little differently, we have a conversation about it. But that's all it ever is, a conversation. I never get mad at my employees for making customers happy, and they know it. I have their backs. This gives them real power, and they have no fear that their jobs are ever in jeopardy because they did "too much" to satisfy a customer. That attitude translates right through to the customers.

The flip side of this strategy is that employees, when in a difficult customer situation, will often try to protect the company and their employer first. However, more often than not, the employee will do just enough to keep the situation from getting worse, and that puts the employee at odds with the very successful strategy of creating happy customers and raving fans. To help my team understand this concept, I tell them that I am willing to absorb a short-term profit loss in exchange for a long-term profit explosion! Happy employees make happy customers, and vice versa. It's a win-win scenario.

Sticky Note:
**"You get the best effort from others not by lighting a fire
beneath them, but by building a fire within."**
—Bob Nelson, best-selling author and motivational speaker

Here's a customer service story that goes right to the heart of employee empowerment. A traveler rented a car from a nationally known car rental agency. She arrived at the counter ready to start a vacation, was given the rental contract, and told in which aisle and stall to find her car. When she got to the car, there was another man putting suitcases into the trunk, and his wife was already sitting in the passenger seat. They compared contracts to see if one of them was at the wrong car, but indeed, the license plate designations on both contracts were the same. The rental agency had rented them the exact same vehicle.

So they walked back to the customer service desk to rectify the situation. Both were a bit put off by the error and anxious to begin their respective vacations. When the agent reviewed the documents and saw the company's error, he took immediate action. He asked if anyone had put their luggage into the car yet, and the man said that he had. The agent's reply: "Okay, sir, you take that car."

The man replied that his wife noticed a non-smoking placard on the dashboard and that they'd specifically requested a car in which they could smoke. The agent's reply? Without missing a beat: "Disregard the placard, sir. I'll remove the non-smoking designation from that car when you return it."

Bingo. There was an immediate resolution, because the employee was empowered to make that decision. No need to clear it with headquarters or try to reach his manager. No phone calls had to be made. The employee was empowered to do whatever it took to immediately solve the problem, and the agent took his next empowered step to accommodate the woman's delay: He offered a free upgrade with a few bells and whistles thrown in to make up for her inconvenience. Again, no need to check with his manager. He was empowered to create happy customers. He did.

Cross-Training and Incentives

Cross-training employees is another way to empower them. In the bike business, I cross-trained mechanics to help on the sales floor, so that when we were extremely busy, customers weren't waiting. Having employees walk a few steps in each other's shoes helps them appreciate the jobs their co-workers do, but more importantly, it contributes to customers getting the best possible experience.

It puts everyone in the same boat, rowing in the same direction—achieving customer satisfaction and creating happy customers and raving fans.

> ### *Sticky Note:*
> Nothing is obvious to the uniformed! Keep this in mind when cross-training employees. Never make assumptions about what they know. Make sure employees who do not usually interact with customers know exactly what to say and do.

When I'm cross-training employees about over-the-top customer service, I relate this story: A customer came in to my bike shop, carrying a tire pump (the thin, portable type that mounts on the bike frame), and I could read on his face that he was steaming mad. I could also see that the pump had a bend in it, which meant it probably fell off his bike and he ran over it. As he approached the counter, he said, "This pump stinks, it's defective…" and on and on he went in a raised voice, and with a few curse words thrown in. I let him finish venting (very important). Then I asked his name.

"Tom."

"Tom, the first thing I want you to know is that I'm going to make sure you leave here a happy, satisfied customer. Is that fair?"

"Yes."

"Okay, but first, Tom (using a customer's name is important), I need to ask you a favor. Would that be okay?"

"Yes."

"Great. I need to ask that you and I have a normal conversation without shouting and swearing. Can we do that, please?"

"Yes."

"Okay, Tom, please tell me what happened so that I understand."

He explained that the pump fell off, and he ran over it. I immediately suggested that, possibly, either we didn't mount it correctly (not likely, but possible) or, if he mounted it himself, perhaps he didn't have the mounting brackets on tight enough. Not waiting for his answer, I then offered to give him a brand-new pump. "Would that be okay with you?"

"Absolutely."

Tom was somewhat taken aback but clearly pleased, almost to the point of being stunned in disbelief!

I further offered to mount the new pump for him, but he did not have the bike with him, so I took the time to explain exactly how to adjust the mounting bracket to avoid the same problem from happening again. Tom said he understood, and that he really appreciated my efforts.

"Is there anything else I can do to make this a great experience for you?"

"Nope. You've been more than fair and have done more than I actually thought you would."

Was the problem our fault? Maybe. Was it the customer's fault? Maybe. The point is, a $20 pump cost me $8 to $10 (you never really invest the full retail, although you want to be sure that you're portraying your solution at the full retail price). Even if it was his fault, my total cost investment (*investment*, not expense) was low. That small amount ensured that this customer left both fully satisfied and as a raving fan.

The flip side would have had Tom leaving in one of two ways: 1) he would still be angry, or 2) he would think the experience was okay but he wouldn't be impressed. It would have been just another shopping experience.

I explain to employees that when customers, like Tom, went back to their cars, they probably admitted to themselves that they were, in fact, wrong (Tom knocked the pump out, and the father knew his kid hit a curb and bent the wheel), but they thought to themselves, "They took care of me anyway!" In both cases, their consciences probably got the better of them. What happens next? They bring their business back to the store!

Here's how I looked at this situation.

Tom came in angry and vented his anger to me—this is the equivalent of a broken plate.

After letting him vent, I told him that I would take care of the situation and make it right—I gathered up the plate's broken pieces.

I gave him a new pump and offered to install it, all for free—the pieces of the plate are now assembled back together.

I thanked Tom and told him how much I valued his business—this is like putting glue all over the broken plate so that it is once again strong and dependable.

Most bike shops would have tried to diagnose what caused the pump to fall off the bike, and, upon learning that Tom installed it incorrectly, they probably would have tried to charge him for a new pump. Some "forward-thinking" stores may have tried to do what they perceived to be either right or fair by selling Tom a new pump at a discount, or perhaps at the store's cost, thinking they were doing Tom a favor while protecting the business from a loss in profit due to a situation that was no fault of their own.

Now that you see both sides of the situation, let me ask you a question. Which approach do you think will most ensure that Tom will both spend more in the store and refer his friends? Glue works every time.

Every one of your employees should know that you want them to do whatever it takes to create happy customers and raving fans.

Politeness Packs 'Em In

Impoliteness can never be tolerated. It's the fastest way to lose a customer.

About twenty years ago, our family's VCR broke. There were three stores in close proximity. I set out with my four kids to buy another one. You couldn't have a houseful of kids without a VCR! We went into the first store, and there were only about three customers in the store. A clerk was standing behind the counter, and I stood there for about ten minutes. In all that time, he never once looked up and acknowledged me...not one time in ten minutes! Granted, I wasn't there to spend a lot, but he didn't know that! After about fifteen minutes, I said, "Excuse me," and was promptly met with, "Sir, I'm already waiting on a customer, and have one more waiting. I can only wait on one at a time."

So I replied, "Well, I'll make it easy on you then. Come on, kids, we're going." Of course, they immediately complained that they wanted a VCR, and I assured them they'd get one, but not at that store.

As we drove to the next store, I explained to my kids that as consumers, people have choices as to where they spend their hard-earned money. And, not treated properly, customers can "vote with their feet and cross the street!" My kids have never forgotten this lesson. Obviously, the better approach for this clerk would have been for him to simply acknowledge me when I walked up to the counter with the simple sentence, "I'll be with you just as soon as I can. I'm waiting on someone else at the moment. I appreciate your patience." Such a statement probably would have bought him another fifteen minutes of my time.

Do you think such impoliteness will punch holes into that store's bucket? You bet it will. Like I did, other customers will go

Sticky Note:
Remember this:
All customers have the ability to "vote with their feet and cross the street."

somewhere else where politeness will pack customers in.

Employees with over-the-top customer-service attitudes and empowerment are the best glue ever!

Sticking Points:

Here's the recap of the important points to remember about the best customer service strategies that ensure great customer stick:

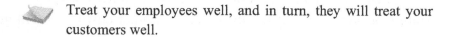 Treat your employees well, and in turn, they will treat your customers well.

Empowerment rocks. It's that simple.

Nothing is obvious to the uniformed. Remember that when you're training employees about great service techniques.

Be certain your employees know they can do whatever it takes to make customers happy. Do not worry about "giving away the shop."

Cross-training employees is another way to empower them, and it contributes to customers getting the best possible experience.

Politeness packs customers in.

If this book had only room for one sentence, it would be this: **Happy customers who become raving fans are the surest way to a successful, profitable business.**

Chapter Five:
It's All about Longevity

Keeping Customers for Life

Think about your favorite glue again. One of its characteristics may be that it grabs and holds things quickly, but it's probably also your favorite because it holds things together forever. It's doesn't dry out, leaving you with broken pieces again after a few months. It lasts.

Getting customers to stick with you works the same way. You want to get them and keep them, especially now that you know the importance of their lifetime values.

Go the Extra Mile

It's said, "There are never any traffic jams on the extra mile." Going the extra mile for your customers is one of the single best ways to keep your customers glued for life.

As we discussed earlier, we've all, sadly, come to expect lousy customer service. That said, if you "inspect what you expect," act on any negative reports immediately, evaluate your policies (especially your Ivory-Tower policies), and provide over-the-top customer service, you'll already be ahead of your competition. But why stop there? Go the extra mile. It's becoming easier to really stand out without a ton of effort.

Sticky Note:

A change in mindset: The minute a customer starts to ask "Can you...?" your mind should be focused on thinking about "How can I...?" and trying to provide the extra "something" for free, if at all possible. The extra "wow" that you create will be far more valuable than the extra expense.

I often speak to entrepreneurs about newsletter marketing. On one of my trips to Florida, Steve Clark, the host of the meeting, went a few extra steps out of his way to make certain to check that my hotel accommodations were memorable by upgrading me to a suite. I thought that was a nice touch, but when I got to my room, I found he'd also left a gift basket for me. After a long day of travel and speaking, it certainly put a smile on my face.

It also got me to really thinking about the power of this business philosophy about going the extra mile, and it solidified in my mind the positive benefits of doing so.

Going the extra mile can make all the difference for your business.

By the way, I was so touched by Steve going the extra mile, that when I landed at the Philadelphia airport, I got out my camera (which I always carry with me) and shot a video about the trip for my Web TV program called Newsletter Guru TV (www.NewsletterGuru.TV). The episode was called "That Little Something Extra," and in it, I mentioned Steve and his company by name.

See what I mean? It doesn't take much to get people singing your praises! So the question is: Are you giving your customers something to sing about?

Sticky Note:
With the sorry state of customer service these days, it's so easy to set yourself apart by traveling the extra mile. Customers will appreciate it and reward you with repeat business.

If you're not sure, here are two easy ways your business can go the extra mile:

- Surprise customers with little extras—perks and bonuses that make them feel special and valued. They create positive feelings. Your customers will remember them and feel good about doing business with your company. Most of all, they're going to tell others about their great experience.

- If you've got an Internet company, send them an extra "special" report, or perhaps bonus them with a surprise MP3 recording. Or mail a book or some kind of surprise gift to your best clients.

Every once in a while, go the extra mile, especially for your better customers, and it will definitely put a smile on their faces.

Sure, it might take a few dollars and a bit of your time, but it *more* than it pays for itself, over and over. Plus, you won't have to worry about the competition. Remember, there's never a traffic jam on the extra mile.

Cuff 'Em

Another way to ensure customer longevity is to "handcuff" them to your business. There are a variety of ways to do this, but let me warn you first: you *must* support these efforts with outstanding customer service, or your efforts can quickly backfire!

The more you do for your customers, the more difficult it becomes for them to walk away from your business. The more

ingrained you can get into your customers' businesses, the more likely they're going to stick with you long-term.

The key is to determine what you can offer them that your competitors cannot. The closer you can get to the core of their operations, the more you "handcuff" them to you. I also refer to this as the "pain of disconnect."

Building your relationships with customers is a simple way to politely "handcuff" them to you.

- Take the time and effort to *learn about their operations*. After all, if they eventually consider choosing a new vendor, they'll be faced with re-explaining, re-teaching, and imparting all that information about their business that you already know to someone else. Knowing they'll have to invest that time and effort tends to make the idea of changing vendors less attractive.

- *Work with them in the role of a consultant* as opposed to a mere order taker. If you are your customers' consultant in addition to their vender, it becomes tougher for them to walk away. What are some ways you and your team members could function as consultants?

Again, if you manage to "handcuff" them, but fail to support it with solid customer service and performance, you will create a lot of resentment and a very displeased customer.

Conversely, if you've been supporting them all along with outstanding customer service, it isn't likely that they'll go looking for a new vendor, and they will appreciate you in the role of their consultant.

> ***Sticky Note:***
> **"Giving is better than receiving because giving starts the receiving process." —Jim Rohn, leading motivational speaker, philosopher, and entrepreneur**

Reciprocity is another psychologically persuasive means of building stronger customer relationships long-term. Like the idea of "handcuffing" them, this one also carries a warning: Give, but *expect nothing in return.*

Reciprocity goes hand-in-hand with the idea of going the extra mile for customers. When you do something extra for them, they'll remember it, and psychologically might feel like they should return the favor by giving you extra business.

Like I said: Never expect a return, and by all means, *never ever* suggest to them that they do a favor in return.

This no-strings-attached mentality is a key factor in gaining the benefit of reciprocity.

In their book "*Yes! 50 Scientifically Proven Ways to Be Persuasive,*" authors Goldstein, Martin, and Cialdini described a study about hotel guests reusing their towels. The study measured guests' receptivity to reusing towels rather than receiving fresh ones each day.

Some guests saw a placard in their bathrooms, suggesting that a donation to an environmental organization *would* be made if they opted to reuse towels. Other guests saw placards that indicated donations *had already been made* on their behalf.

The first version had strings attached (i.e., *if* you reuse your towel, we'll make a donation); the second one had no strings attached (i.e., we've made a donation on behalf of our guests). The rate of towel reuse by the no-strings-attached guests was considerably higher.

Be a resource to your customers. Your product or service might not be able to meet all of your customers' needs. When that happens, try to find someone who can. They'll appreciate the information, and don't worry about losing them. While they may go somewhere else for the thing you can't offer, if you've provided killer customer service, they'll certainly be back. Plus, the reciprocity factor kicks again in these situations. You do them a

favor by providing a resource, so they'll probably want to pay that back. At the end of the day, your bank account will always be bigger, not smaller, for providing your customers with other resources.

The bottom line to keeping customers for life is as simple as the golden rule. Treat your customers the way you'd like to be treated. By *really* serving your customers, you cement the foundations of your relationships with them, and they'll stick like glue...and stay with you for the long haul.

Sticking Points:

Here's the recap of the important points to remember about the secrets to longevity, getting and keeping customers for life:

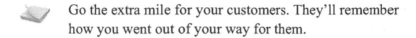 Go the extra mile for your customers. They'll remember how you went out of your way for them.

Politely "handcuff" your customers to you, but be certain to support this technique with rock-solid service.

The more ingrained you can get into your customers' businesses, the more likely they're going to stick with you.

Learn about your customers' operations.

Become your customers' consultant.

Make use of reciprocity. Give, but expect nothing in return.

Over-the-top happy customers and raving fans pay off!

Chapter Six:
True Blue

Selling More to Current Customers

As I mentioned in the beginning of this book, there are only two ways to grow your business. Get more customers, or sell more to the ones you already have. It's really just that simple.

I'm certain you're interested in growing your business since you're reading this book in the first place. Right? Of course. And you're quickly understanding the importance of sticking like glue.

So how do you sell more to current customers?

Analyze your customer list and learn who's spending the most. If you want to sell more (and who doesn't?) these are these easiest people to sell to since you already have an established and trusting relationship with them, *and* your cost of doing business with them is the lowest.

High sales and low cost always equates to greater profitability. It's one of the simplest equations in business. So, know who your hyper-responsive customers are, and use that to your advantage.

Marketing legend, and one of my business mentors, Dan Kennedy, puts it this way, "If you want to sell more, go back to the people that have already identified themselves as buyers—your customers—because buyers are buyers are buyers!"

Not only are your current customers—the water in your bucket—more likely to buy from you, more importantly, they actually *want* to buy more from you. They've proven themselves to be hyper-responsive, so take advantage of that! Since they want to buy more from you, *you need to have more ways to sell to them.*

This is especially important during tough economic times. When customers are tightening their belts and keeping a closer watch on every dollar they spend, they're much more hesitant to spend their money with someone they don't "know, like, and trust." However, with the really good glue you've developed through over-the-top customer service, going the extra mile, and cuffing them to you, they're much more likely to spend their money with you because they know, like, and trust you.

Let me tell you one of the ways that we sold more to our existing bike shop customers. It is customary for most bike shops to offer a free thirty-day checkup with every new bike purchase. Essentially, the manufacturers encourage this to make any adjustments necessary to the brakes and gears as a result of cables stretching from initial use. The thirty-day "mini tune-up" would take about twenty minutes to complete.

The truth is that most bike shops hoped that their customers would not remember to bring the bike in so that it didn't jam up their service department with work that did not bring in any revenue. We did just the opposite! We mailed our customers a personal letter thirty days after their purchase, reminding them to bring their bikes back in, and we even listed the reasons why it was important.

Guess what happened? Every time customers brought their bikes back, we got another chance to wow them with our exceptional service and attention to detail. Guess what else we did? While the bike was being tuned up, a salesman would show the customer around the store, explaining some additional accessory items that might make their cycling experience even more enjoyable—and, oh by the way, we'd be happy to install these accessories while their bikes were in the shop! Think about how you can develop such a strategy in your business.

Here's a recent story I'll share with you about a very creative way to sell more to your existing customers: With my busy speaking schedule, I recently purchased a few new suits, and the salesman told me that as a customer, I was entitled to free alterations for life. Wow! As someone whose weight has gone up and down (a little!), this is a great benefit. The salesman then asked me if I traveled much and if my suits came back wrinkled. Yes and yes!

He told me that, as a valued customer, I can also get free steam pressing of my suits, and, get this—with same day service! Another wow! If you're like me, you've probably had your suits dry-cleaned after a road trip just because they're wrinkled, not dirty. I was already thrilled with the sale price I received for the suits, but these two added benefits left me feeling very committed to this store. From the store's prospective, mission accomplished— another more-than-satisfied customer!

As entrepreneurs and business owners, one of our greatest challenges is to find ways to encourage customers to buy more often (repeat business) and tell others about our company (referrals). Think about how brilliant this clothing store's strategy is. Let's face it, everyone's weight changes, and when customers bring in their suits for alterations, chances are high that they'll make additional purchases, perhaps a new shirt or two! Steam pressing is also a no-brainer for the company. The service probably takes less than ten minutes to perform, and they have a customer in their store twice, once dropping off and then again picking up. It's probably a safe assumption that a business traveler usually owns more than one suit and is more inclined to pick up a new tie, belt, or perhaps a few shirts while there.

Finally, let us not overlook the incredible bonus of satisfied customers, like me, telling a lot of people about my experience, which I've done repeatedly and like I'm doing right now. Customer service today is so bad that when a business does anything to standout favorably, people are surprised and are usually happy to share their experience with others.

By the way, my new favorite men's store is Men's Warehouse®! By the way again, I've now told this story to thousands of people through social media and now in this book. Standout customer service works!

I simply can't overstate what a big hurdle you'll overcome simply by getting a new customer to purchase from you just once. With all of the effort invested in this initial, single transaction, you owe it to your business to maximize the profit of each and every new customer relationship.

What are some new ways you can sell more to your current customers?

All Customers Are Not Created Equal

Here's something I'd like you to repeat after me: "All customers are not created equal." Once again, "All customers are not created equal." Remember that. It goes back to the 80/20 rule: 80 percent of your profits comes from 20 percent of your customers. Knowing that fact, why would anyone *not* cater to that 20 percent?

Every customer should receive great customer service, but those who are more loyal, deserve more.

This is the basis for rewards programs, like those offered by the airlines and restaurants.

When you travel exclusively with one airline, you build up more miles, and the more miles you get, the more perks you get. Customers who have more miles are treated differently, treated better, and there's nothing wrong with that.

These programs don't arbitrarily play favorites. They simply reward loyalty.

Those travelers who are packed into economy class, and jammed into the middle seat, are as eligible to sit in first class as those who are doing so. They simply have to spend more and earn more miles.

Loyalty programs are great ways to reward your best customers.

Catering to your best customers starts with the 80/20 rule, but it continues to the 90/10 and even the 95/5 rules. No matter how you slice it, the greatest percentage of your sales (and ultimately your profits!) comes from the smallest percentage of your customer base.

When you cater to your best 20 percent, you're not slighting the other 80 percent. Like the airline miles rewards program, anyone can sit in first class if they've got enough miles. The same thing applies here.

Remember, your customer list is your most valuable asset. Knowing how to segregate and create specific marketing programs for specific groups of customers is one of the smartest and easiest ways to grow your business and increase your profits.

Sticky Note:

The 80/20 Rule: 80% of your profits come from 20% of your customers. They're the easiest to sell to and they generate higher profit margins. This is the single greatest reason to focus efforts on customer retention.

Understanding Customer Loyalty Programs

Think about yourself as a consumer. Do you collect airline miles? Do you get bonus points for refunds by using one credit card instead of another? What about store programs? Do you have bonus cards for a particular grocery store or pharmacy? I know some people who carry more of those store key-chain cards on their key rings than keys! Maybe you're one of them. All of these examples are testaments to how well these programs work.

As the consumer, you benefit from these loyalty programs by getting discounts and special perks. These programs help to shape your future buying habits.

A quick example. A few days ago, my son, Nick, received a promotion at work and needed to set up a home office. Stephanie and I said that we would do this for him as a congratulations gift. While there are many office store options, Office Max® is where we went. Why? Because they regularly send me these discount cards to reward me for my business. With most pricing being extremely competitive between the major chains, the 15 percent discount card made it very easy for me to say to Nick, "Meet me at Office Max®!"

For the companies, these programs also provide the opportunity to collect valuable data that allows them to cater to individual customers.

Every time you find yourself selecting one store or company over another because of your desire to build up rewards points, you can remind yourself that these loyalty programs work.

If you've been playing the game, you've also come to realize that sticking with one store or company pays off much quicker than having bonus cards with several competing entities.

Take, for example, frequent flier programs. Let's say you fly 25,000 miles each year, and 25,000 miles can be cashed in for a free ticket. All things being equal, it makes sense to use a single airline to build up your miles rather than traveling with several different carriers and watering down each program you're participating in. That is the very crux of loyalty programs. They encourage you to build points with one to the exclusion of the competitors.

A big caveat to these programs working successfully long-term is that loyalty programs must be easy to understand and use, for your customers and your staff.

Here's what I mean. Last year, I was drawn in to a particular airline's frequent flier program, because, on the surface, it seemed quite simple—gather up airline miles and get a free flight. Not so fast! After I accumulated almost 90,000 miles, more than enough for two tickets, Stephanie and I tried to book our free flight. The bottom line was that unless we both had the same birthday, or were willing to take separate flights on separate days, or unless we were willing to travel to different destinations, we were not able to use to the free tickets.

Needless to say, this royally ticked me off, so much so that I cancelled the frequent flyer credit card, and I swear I will not use this airline again!

I've shared this story with friends, and, without surprise, they've had similar experiences. Talk about a total backfire! My suggestion is that unless you're prepared to actually reward your customers for their loyalty, and make it super easy for them to be rewarded, don't bother setting up such a system, because it will do a huge amount of damage to your reputation.

Done correctly, however, loyalty programs are an excellent way to glue your customers to you for life.

Are loyalty clubs a lot of work to establish and administer? I'll be honest: Yes! They *are* a lot of work. Are they worth it? Yes! Make that a resounding YES! Consider this. Statistics show that customers belonging to a loyalty program patronize businesses, on average, twice as often, and spend four times as much money.

Twice as often, *four* times as much money. Do you think that impacts your customers' lifetime values? Of course it does. Take advantage of that. Nobody ever said running a growing and profitable business is easy, but remember this: Getting current customers to spend more with you is easier and more profitable than getting new customers. Your loyalty program can grease the skids for it.

All customers are not created equal, and that very notion is reason enough to establish a loyalty program. You want to encourage those who spend more with you to...well, spend *even more*. The best part is that they're very likely going to do just that.

Gaining Entrance

Those who spend the most with you deserve your best offers, promotions, and rewards. As I said, there's nothing wrong with that thinking and approach. Do they let every person who buys an airline ticket into the Admiral's Lounge? No, they don't. How does the airline determine who gets in and who doesn't? They track miles and purchases with affiliates. It's a lot of work, but I assure you, it's worth it to them, or they wouldn't do it.

Dangling perks as a means to increase revenue is an effective marketing technique. Picture the harried business traveler. He's finally gotten to the airport after an intense meeting, dealt with security procedures, and is ready to spend some quiet time at the gate prior to departure. Oops—there's a vacationing family with a screaming toddler and antsy five-year-old waiting for the same flight. Across the hall, he sees a quiet sanctuary. The Admiral's Club. It's an attractive benefit that just might garner his loyalty in order to join.

If he spends more with the airline, he can gain admission. And he can get there faster by patronizing the airline exclusively, by being loyal. Not only will he be loyal, he's going to improve his lifetime value to the airline, and he'll probably end up supporting that earlier statistic—fly with them twice as often (if not more) and spend four times as much.

Establishing—and Benefitting from—Your Customer Loyalty Program

I've told you honesty that loyalty programs are a lot of work, and they are, but they are clearly worth it. In fact, loyalty programs are one of the best methods you can use to plug the holes in your leaky bucket. Those customers who see value in repeat purchases because of the special offers, promotions, and rewards that they receive are going to stick around in your bucket. They're not going to leak out. Again, this presumes you provide a solid product or service and back that up with over-the-top customer service, and are easy to do business with.

You need to study your customer list and data, and figure out who should get what as a reward. Slice and dice your list and create separate offers and mailings to different levels based on your customers' spending histories. Would you even consider sending the same offer or promotion to the guy who spends five bucks with you once a year as the guy who buys every month and spends a total of $10,000 annually? No, of course you wouldn't. Or you *shouldn't*! If you do, you need to revamp that approach in a hurry or risk alienating your best clients.

Sticky Note:
Statistically, loyalty program customers visit twice as often and spend four times more than customers who don't belong.

You can find a number of turnkey loyalty programs with a quick Internet search. You can go it alone if you'd like, but you don't have to. Remember, success leaves tracks. Look for loyalty reward programs that have already been established and are working successfully in other industries, and adapt them to your business. If you've got hundreds of transactions each week, you may determine that a "canned" program is worth every penny to you. The loyalty program seller offers membership cards and does all the tracking for you by storing the data that's collected in an online repository.

Whether you do your own tracking or pay someone else to do it for you, it's imperative that you actually do something with the data you collect. If you don't, you're simply wasting everyone's time (including your own), and you're wasting your money. Additionally, you'll begin to alienate your customers if you collect information that you never act on. Instead, use your customer loyalty program to benefit your customers *and* your business. Consider this scenario.

Let's take a look out our frequent flier again. He's learned the value of loyalty, and after his experience with the screaming toddler and antsy five-year-old, he quickly joined the airline's program to enjoy the perks of the Admiral's Club. The airline has a joint venture partner with a particular hotel chain, so he's sure to always book with them in order to continue to leverage his benefits in the loyalty program.

Upon his first reservation, he answers several questions. They ask what type of room he prefers, on what floor, which complimentary newspaper he'd like, and whether or not he uses the airport shuttle service. When he calls to make another reservation, he's asked the very same questions. Shame on the hotel! They've collected incredibly valuable data, but they've done nothing with it. They've wasted our frequent flier's time by forcing him to answer the same questions with every subsequent reservation. Since they've got all the information, here's how his reservation phone call should play out:

"Thanks for calling, Mr. Jones. For the dates you're requesting, we've got a room on the second floor with a king-sized bed. Also, if you provide your flight times, I'll go ahead and schedule you for the shuttle right now. Plus we'll have a copy of *USA Today*® waiting for you."

That just scratches the surface of what they can do with the data they have. In addition, the hotel can continue to build their information about Mr. Jones' preferences by tracking what he selects on each visit and *using* the data. For example, by tracking what he selects from the minibar, they can personalize it for his next visit. If he purchased his favorite beverage, his minibar should be stocked with twice as much of that product on his next visit. Will he buy twice as much? Maybe not, but at least the hotel is providing him with the option.

Imagine his impression if he's greeted at registration with this conversation. "Welcome, Mr. Jones. May I make a reservation for you for breakfast, as usual, in our dining room tomorrow morning?" You see, Mr. Jones always eats breakfast in the dining room. The hotel has that information. By putting it to use and personalizing Mr. Jones' experience, they continue to make him feel special and increase his loyalty.

Let's take this example one step farther. Mr. Jones has a less-than-stellar experience with this hotel in a particular city. He probably won't forego his relationship with them over it (unless, of course, it becomes a trend). Why? Because he's invested a lot of time "training" the hotel about his preferences. He always gets the exact type of room in the location he wants with his preferred newspaper and a breakfast reservation, without having to ask. He'll probably be willing to give them a pass on a single bad experience rather than start over with another hotel chain.

The hotel has "hand-cuffed" themselves to Mr. Jones. He will try hard to avoid the pain of disconnect and starting from scratch with a new hotel chain. If he happens to mention the bad experience, the hotel should do whatever it can to make it up to him. Why? Lifetime value. Both the customer and the business benefit from the loyalty program.

If you happen to use a store's bonus card, you know they're collecting a veritable gold mine of information about your every purchase. The sharpest marketers are putting this data to excellent use. You'll get coupons and offers that are customized to you and your buying habits. For example, if you purchase baby formula, the store with a strong marketing department is going to start sending you baby food coupons in about a year. Likewise, the florist who knows you buy flowers on a particular date every year can be very proactive with offers and bonuses to help ensure that you're going to repeat your purchase…with them.

Some companies miss the boat on this approach and send the same coupons and offers to every customer. If I've never purchased pet food, why send me coupons for it? Conversely, if I regularly buy a particular brand, why not send me coupons for the store's competitive product? Maybe I'll switch and purchase their product with a higher profit margin for the company. Use the data you have to improve the amount your best customers spend with you.

Make It Personal

Like the hotel example in which they tracked Mr. Jones's selections from the minibar and boosted sales by stocking it with his regular preferences, continue to build on the data you collect about your customers. There are many customer relationship management software programs that automate the process for you. Why track what your customers are buying if you're not going to use it?

That's the beauty of loyalty programs. You provide special perks to your customers for their loyalty (along with their increased spending), and in turn, they provide you with data that signals their preferences and buying habits. It's information that you can leverage to increase the amount they spend with you.

If you've got customers who make the same purchase at the same time month after month, you can offer to automate the whole process. Today's technology does most of the work. Offer them special pricing and perhaps free shipping. You keep their credit card on file and ship the product as scheduled. They get what they want and need with no effort on their part; you get continued sales with effectively no effort on your part.

There's a lot of other data you can collect through your loyalty program that you can put to use. If you know customers' birthdays, why not send a special offer? More often than not, your customer spends more than the amount of that special offer. Have you ever been in a restaurant's birthday club? They usually offer free dessert on your birthday. If you take advantage of it, do you simply stop in for a piece of cake? Of course not. You buy the meal first…and you're probably not celebrating alone!

Loyalty programs are work, but they pay off handsomely. With the power of technology, there is no reason not to put one in place for your business. With a little investigating and a few calculations regarding your return on investment, I believe you will quickly agree…and you'll take a giant step in strengthening your glue with your True Blue customers, and improving your profitability!

Additional Perks

Here are additional ways you can reward your best customers for their loyalty:

- Let your best customers know that they are your best customers.
- Give them a shorter line to wait in.
- Give them different VIP cards.
- Promote them in your monthly customer newsletter.

Give your True Blue customers over-the-top perks, and make them your raving fans!

Sticking Points:

Here's the recap of the important points to remember about customer loyalty programs:

 All customers are not created equal. Reward those who provide you with more business.

 Think about yourself as a consumer. You're probably in some sort of loyalty program. Why? Because they work!

 Loyalty programs are a lot of work, but they pay off. Remember your customer's lifetime value before dismissing the idea of creating a loyalty program.

 Loyalty program customers visit twice as often and spend four times as much. They are your most profitable customers.

 Those who spend the most with you deserve the best offers and promotions. These specials "dangle the carrot" in front of others and are often the impetus they need to join.

 Use the data you collect, or why bother collecting it? If you don't use it, you'll waste time and money and alienate your customers.

 Personalize it! The more you personalize your offers and promotions, the more likely your customer is going to be to buy.

Chapter Seven:
Referrals Rock!

Creating Your Customer Referral Program

You've already learned that there's a lot more profit in selling to your existing customers than in getting new ones (not that new ones aren't important). It's simple: it's easier to sell to folks who know you, because you've already cleared what Zig Ziglar calls the no-trust hurdle. I heard marketing legend, Dan Kennedy, say one time that if you want to sell more, go to the people who have already identified themselves as buyers—your customers! I agree, and I'll let you in on a secret: referrals are the next best thing!

Compared to the usually high cost of acquiring a new customer, there's a much lower cost of acquisition with a referral, because they find you; you don't have to go prospecting for them. This is a huge marketing advantage.

Remember my story about Joe and the billiard table? Thanks to his being over-the-top happy with our service, Joe referred us to his friends and neighbors. I know that in just one season, at least two more customers walked through the door and purchased pool tables. "I don't know exactly what I want, but Joe said I'd be crazy not to shop here." This example goes back many years, but if my memory is correct, I also believe that price was not an issue as, again, they were pre-sold. That kind of advertising is tough, if not impossible, to buy.

Word-of-mouth advertising and referrals occur because of over-the-top, out-of-the-ballpark, put-gigantic-smiles-on-their-faces kind of customer service. There's no doubt in my mind about that. I've seen it time and time again, and it's added to my bank account time and time again.

That's why I believe in serving my customers and going the extra mile every time. When you do, you create raving fans that can end up selling your product or service better than your own sales staff can. Trust me. Joe became one of my best salesmen, and he didn't draw a salary or benefits!

While incredible customer service goes a long way in generating referrals, you don't have to leave them to chance. A formal customer referral program can really be one of your greatest marketing tools. It's not enough to get referrals like Joe's. Word-of-mouth referrals are excellent, but you can do even better by offering a referral rewards program. Let me share of few examples.

My wife, Stephanie, is the director of a large child-care facility, and her company offers a free week of tuition for any referral she gets from a parent. A free week is a pretty big deal— child care is expensive. I think it's a great offer.

I also know of a very successful insurance company that sends out a monthly customer newsletter (a smart idea!), and without fail, every month they include a front-page picture and the name of the monthly referral program winner along with a picture of the prize: a flat-screen TV. That's right. Every month they give away a flat-screen TV to the client who refers the most new business to them.

You may think that's extravagant, but think about the math and remember the lifetime value! Let's say each insurance customer has a lifetime value of $2500 (probably a low estimate). If they get five referrals a month from their customer base of 1000 clients, that adds up to $12,500. They can buy a flat-screen TV for about ten percent of that. They're certainly getting a great return on their investment. Would this insurance company do as well if their monthly prize was a free pizza? I think not.

Some business owners I talk with tend to choke at this idea. "I'm not giving away a flat-screen TV every month. I'll offer the winner a 10 percent discount instead." Ugh. That kind of offer is going to do very little to motivate your customers to remember your name or pick up the phone and make a referral. At least the child-care operator offers 25 percent, which has a real impact for her clients. They use the service week in and week out.

Remember: Small thinking gets small results. Think big and get big results!

My good friend and business partner, Bobby Deraco, owns Synapse Print Management. Synapse prints all of my corporate newsletters, my books (including this one), and they also handle the printing and mailing for my very popular Concierge Print and Mail On Demand Service (www.NewsletterPrintingService.com). Recently, I got both an e-mail and a large postcard from Synapse, promoting that they would be giving away iPhones® and iPads® as referral prizes. That was one e-mail that I was sure to save. In fact, I called Bobby to congratulate him on thinking big, as the iPad™ was the very hot new item at the time.

Your referral reward has got to be enough of an incentive to get folks to play along. When the incentive is great enough, your customers will go out of their way to make a referral rather than simply mentioning your product or service in passing.

By the way, Bobby told me told me that the iPad® promotion got the attention of many customers and prospects. In fact, his company landed a new client on their first meeting, generated over $10K in immediate revenue ($4,600+ in profit which more than paid for the iPad), and they're now working closely with this new client on a $100K annual contract deal.

Again, the big lesson here is that big thinking yields big results.

The insurance company I told you about even goes one step farther. They offer an annual prize as well—four days and three nights to a Caribbean destination for two. That really gets an "Oh wow!" response when people hear about it. The cost of the trip for two runs about $1000 for the company. Again, remember lifetime value before you dismiss the idea as too expensive for your business. A flat-screen TV and the chance to win a trip to the Bahamas motivate a lot of people to make referrals.

When you create your customer referral program, first keep in mind that *you've got to make it worth your customer's time to participate.* Unfortunately, many entrepreneurs are too cheap when it comes to their referral programs. Let me be blunt with you here, just as I am with the entrepreneurs whom I coach: Offering your customers a 10 percent discount on a future purchase is about as exciting as watching paint dry; it's not going to do the job! A free ticket to the movies or a free ice cream at the local ice cream parlor is just not enough to make most people go to the time and trouble of referring you.

The reward has got to be substantial. If the cost is a sticking point for you, go back and look at the lifetime value of your customers. As the old saying goes, "You have to spend some money to make money." It's simply a return on your investment, just like every other cost you incur while running your business.

Here's what I suggest you do: Figure out what your average lifetime value of a new customer is. Once you know this number, I predict you will not be so cheap with your customer referral program.

A second key ingredient to creating a referral reward program is that *it must be reasonably simple to understand and use.* In fact, you should be able to explain it in a single sentence. For example, "Get $X (or some other prize) for referring a buying customer." Period.

If you add a bunch of caveats to your program—"The referral must make a purchase on a Tuesday, make a second purchase within thirty days, opt into our mailing list, and purchase at least one item from our value item list"—you won't get many customers making referrals. And you'll drive yourself crazy keeping track of it. This happened to me just the other day. I received a reward from an office supply store that I frequent, and my first thought was "Cool!" Then I started reading the fine print, and I essentially had to jump through so many hoops I threw it in the trash can.

Sticky Note:
When it comes to creating your referral program, there's one basic rule: Keep it simple!

So, in addition to making your program simple to understand, *it must also be simple to administer*. The first always leads to the second. You don't want to create a program that ends up requiring a full-time employee to keep track of everything.

Complex programs can also quickly lead to misunderstandings and dissatisfied customers. "You said that if I did this, I'd get that. Well, I did this and didn't get that!" Not only will you lose the possibility of future referrals, you'll probably lose the original customer. Ouch! That's exactly what you don't want to have happen.

Be certain your employees understand the referral program and can explain it quickly to your customers. If your employees don't understand it, they won't promote it, and if your employees don't understand it, your customers surely won't.

Again, simplicity rules. The idea is to generate business from the next best thing to your existing customer base—a referral.

Your referral program should never be based on luck. That creates distrust, and your customers will be less likely to pick up the phone and make a referral. Don't confuse the examples of the day-care center and insurance company with luck. Not at all. Those programs were based on a contest—the person who generates the most referrals wins.

In the case of the insurance company's end-of-the-year drawing, while there is a bit of luck involved, it is still based on rewarding their customers who make the most referrals. Customers who win more than once during the year improve their chances of winning the end-of-the-year grand prize. In fact, this type of reward program (most referrals in a month wins) is one of the easiest referral programs to create and administer.

Promoting Your Customer Referral Program

But the problem with many referral programs is that they are not regularly promoted. Oh sure, Stephanie, like most good business people, mentions the program to new clients when they initially enroll their child, but most parents forget it minutes after hearing about it. Telling folks about your referral program once is simply not enough.

I had some suggestions on how she should improve her efforts that can work for your business also.

First, I suggested hanging a poster about the referral bonus at the sign-in desk. This way, every day as parents drop off their children, they will be reminded of the one free week with every referral. But don't stop there.

Next, I said she should include a picture of the "Reigning Referral King or Queen" on the poster every month. The picture would include her handing over a giant-sized check for the free week of tuition.

In addition to the poster, I suggested monthly fliers that get inserted into the kids' cubbies with their other belongings. Again, the flier would feature the Reigning Referral King or Queen and the value of the "prize" received for making referrals.

I also suggested that the referral program and the lucky recipients should be featured in the monthly company newsletter.

Why is all of this so important? First of all, because people are crazy-busy and need several reminders. But more importantly, the program works because parents have unlimited contacts with other parents at work, in church, and in their neighborhoods who probably also need child care. The opportunity for new customers by way of referral from happy parents is huge. Granted, Stephanie could only accept a specified number of children, but when she reached capacity, she could start a waiting list. Wow! Can you imagine having a waiting list of customers? With a waiting list, she could practically eliminate her other marketing efforts.

Using a contest for your referral program is a great promotional vehicle. It gives you a reason and opportunity to reach your entire customer base each month to announce the winner. That message does two things. It lets your customers know that, one, you have a referral program and, two, that your referral program is for real and is worthwhile.

In addition, the constant reminders keep your name in front of your customers. Any good sales rep knows the value of having recurring reasons to get in front of customers.

Is setting up and running a formal referral program work? Yep. But can you see how this work can pay huge dividends? I encourage you to give some serious thought to how you can apply such a strategy to your business.

Sticky Note:
Formal referral programs require regular reminders. Remind, remind, and remind them...and then tell them one more time!

U-nique 'Em In!

Remember that childhood joke, "How do you catch a rare rabbit?" "U-nique up on him!" (*You sneak*, in case you didn't get it!)

You can also generate referrals by a unique approach to your business. What's your doctor's office waiting room like? If it's like most, it has a row of chairs with a few scattered end tables that have outdated magazines on them and maybe a television in the corner tuned to an uninteresting talk show. Even a short wait in this environment can seem like an hour. The only mention you might make about the whole ordeal is the time you wasted waiting for your appointment.

Now, imagine a different sort of waiting room, one that has complimentary snacks and beverages, desks and workstations with free Internet hookup or Wi-Fi, and child-care service. Your waiting time may not be any shorter, but it will certainly seem like it is. And chances are good that you're going to speak positively about your experience and tell your friends and neighbors about it. With a little thought and imagination, you can present your business in a unique sort of way that gets your customers talking about their experience and referring others to you.

How can you use a unique, outstanding approach in your business? Dream up new ways to "u-nique 'em in!"

Referrals grow your business. Growing your business makes you more profitable. Once again, I challenge you to think big and get in the referral game! Referrals rock!

Sticking Points:

Here's the recap of the important points to remember about referral programs:

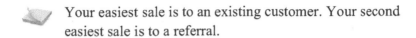 Your easiest sale is to an existing customer. Your second easiest sale is to a referral.

Referrals have a very low cost of acquisition. In essence, they find you; you don't have to prospect for them.

A formal referral program is one of your best marketing tools.

Your program must be simple—simple to explain and simple to administer.

The value of your reward must be worth your customer's time and effort to make the referral and redeem the reward.

Constantly remind your customers about your program and promote it at every opportunity.

Over-the-top customer service and a unique approach to your business are both referral generators.

Chapter Eight:
You're Gonna Need a
Bigger Boat

Testimonials Reel 'Em In!

I love actor Roy Scheider's line in the movie *Jaws*, "We're gonna need a bigger boat!" His character threw large chunks of bait into the water to lure the great white. His eyes went round when he saw what his efforts had produced.

Reel customers in to your business with an equally effective bait: Testimonials. When used right, testimonials can be a key factor in reeling in a boatload of new customers.

Getting and using testimonials is one of the best ways to share the message about how great your product or service is. In fact, marketing guru Dan Kennedy says (I'll paraphrase) that a poorly written but honest testimonial about your company will produce sales infinitely better than the most perfectly crafted sales letter from your marketing department. The latter is you talking about how great you are; the testimonials come from real customers.

Sticky Note:
Testimonials carry infinitely more weight than your most finely worded sales letter. Your customers will relate to like-minded people who promote your company.

One of the surest ways to persuade people to decide in your favor and give you the sale is to show them that other like-minded customers are already doing that. Testimonials are that social proof. So how do you get testimonials? You ask.

Some folks are a bit shy about asking for testimonials. If you fall into that category, let me give you my blunt response: Get over it. You're in business, and testimonials are one of the greatest ways to grow your sales and profits.

Recently, I took a call from a relatively new customer who was calling to tell me that he was thrilled with No Hassle Newsletters and had already gotten some new clients because of it. Nothing makes my day like getting that kind of call, but instead of simply letting it stroke my ego, I put it to work for me—I asked him if he'd jot what he'd just mentioned in an e-mail so that I could include it with the testimonials I already had on my Web site. Plus, I also offered to feature his testimonial (and contact information) in my weekly e-zine—*More Profits and Customers for Life*—that goes out to thousands of subscribers around the world. He was more than happy to oblige.

By the way, if you're not receiving my newsletter—what I refer to as my weekly "multi-media boost for your business"—simply go to www.JimsNewsletter.com and sign up—you'll love it!

While you can get testimonials by asking, you do have to deserve them. That is, if you don't do anything remarkable, no one's going to feel moved to sit down and write you to say "Thanks for simply being average or doing the minimum!" This goes right back to what I covered earlier regarding over-the-top customer service, and the fact that it always pays off for you.

If I had charged the father with the bent bicycle wheel, and then asked for a testimonial about how promptly our technicians fixed his son's bike and how fair the replacement price was, do you think I would have gotten all that extra business? Heck no. Since I offered to replace it at no cost to him and went out of my way to eliminate his pain point, he'd be more inclined to provide a testimonial, and a lot of word-of-mouth publicity.

Most of the testimonials I get, I get because I ask.

Asking for a testimonial during the "honeymoon" phase in a customer relationship is almost always a sure bet that you'll get one. The best time to ask is after an initial positive transaction, or after you've successfully solved your customer's problem and alleviated his or her pain.

But don't limit yourself to that. Acquiring testimonials happens at many different levels. It can appear in your e-mail signature lines, or on every single item you send to your clients. A sentence as simple as "A customer referral is our greatest compliment" works. Or "We love testimonials; tell us how we're doing."

Another way I get testimonials is by having a "testimonial button" on the member site for No Hassle Newsletters. Every time subscribers sign in to the membership site, they see the button, and many have taken the time to click the button and write a testimonial.

Testimonials will lend credibility to your company, but only if they meet certain parameters:

- Never lie or make up testimonials. Prospects can spot fabricated testimonials a mile away!
- If a customer sends you an unprompted testimonial, follow up and ask permission to use your customer's comments.
- If you're asking for the testimonial, you can mention how and where you plan to use it.
- In addition to asking permission, it's important to include your customer's full name, company, or town. "Jim P. from PA" isn't going to do a thing for your credibility. On the other hand, "Jim Palmer, Customer Newsletters, Inc., Exton, PA" is worthwhile. With that information, prospects realize that they could contact "Jim Palmer" directly and

ask about "Jim's" experience. Will they? Probably not, but the fact that they could becomes very persuasive.

- You also want your testimonials to be results-oriented. A testimonial that reads, "Jim's a nice guy and is enjoyable to work with" is nice, but doesn't say very much. A results-oriented one would read: "Jim's newsletter program landed our company three new clients worth $10,000! Newsletters really do work."

Let me show you a great example of a **results-based testimonial** I received from one of my clients:

"Thanks to our No Hassle Newsletter, we were awarded a $400,000 contract!

Tridon Industries has been sending out one of Jim Palmer's No Hassle Newsletters since July 2009. We receive many compliments from our customers regarding the content Jim provides, but the greatest compliment of all was a huge new contract! We recently featured an article about using our Blaze Shield II insulation at the Hershey Hotel & Restaurant. Somehow, an architect in Hawaii received a copy of our newsletter and contacted our offices. After several discussions, we were awarded a $400,000 contract!

Three quick points Jim says about customer newsletters. First, make your newsletter fun and entertaining and not too much about your work. Second, it can take 6-9 months for your newsletter to show some results. And finally, Jim also says that newsletters get passed around. I can attest that he is right on all three counts!

Mary Beth Yannessa
President Tridon Industries, Inc.
Pottstown, PA 19464"

That's the kind of testimonial that is worth its weight in gold. Used correctly, it will help convince prospects that your product or service can also help their business.

I greatly appreciate results-based testimonials, because results-based testimonials speak to the *quality* of the product or service you provide.

However, there is another type of testimonial that is also highly effective, and, given the topic of this book, actually makes me smile even bigger! Here are two examples of **customer-service-based testimonials** that are extremely effective at helping to increase prospective customers' comfort level when considering doing business with your company.

"Jim Palmer is totally focused on you as the customer, and your needs a businessperson or a professional. Whenever we need help (which is often), Jim and his team are there for us. No question is too stupid or mundane. They are simply the best at helping us to support our clients and customers, and to build lasting valuable relationships. Do yourself a favor, and get Jim and No Hassle Newsletters to help you bring additional value to your customers, and additional profits to you and your venture.
David M. Frees Esquire
West Chester, PA"

"The part of your No Hassle Newsletter program that is most impressive to me is the care and commitment to OUR success that is demonstrated by you and your staff. I had a very rocky start with my first couple of newsletters (I don't blame your program), but when I would send up a distress signal to "The Newsletter Guru," I would get an e-mail back in a VERY short time…sometimes from you directly, Jim, and at unusual hours. It blew me away! I sincerely appreciate the attention I was given. On occasion, I asked for "out of the ordinary" assistance, and you generously allowed them to "do whatever it takes" to make it happen. I am very grateful for the friendly and superior assistance I have come to count on. I sincerely recommend "The Newsletter Guru" to any business trying to put together a newsletter.

Sherill Fox

Advanced Ear Care

Laguna Woods, CA"

As I said, customer-service-based testimonials are extremely effective at helping to increase prospective customers' comfort level.

An important point I want to make about testimonials, is that you want to continue to add to your collection of testimonials, especially in light of the fact that you're working so hard on customer retention.

If you've had the same dozen testimonials on your site for the last two years, repeat customers will notice and wonder why no one has said anything lately. Keep asking, and keep updating your testimonials.

A quick legal note about testimonials: The days of inserting the age-old disclaimer "results not typical" are gone. The Federal Trade Commission has updated the guidelines that businesses must follow regarding customer testimonials. You can find "FTC's Guides Concerning the Use of Endorsements and Testimonials in Advertising, which address endorsements by consumers, experts, organizations, and celebrities, as well as the disclosure of important connections between advertisers and endorsers" at http://www.ftc.gov/opa/2009/10/endortest.shtm.

Sticky Note:

Remember: Testimonials must have your customer's full name, company name or town, and be results-oriented in order to be worthwhile.

Use the testimonials in your print advertising, on your Web site, and in your newsletters (more on that in the next chapter!).

Testimonials are excellent bait, proven to reel in new customers. Testimonials grow your business. Before long, you could find yourself in need of a "bigger boat!"

Sticking Points:

Here's the recap of the important points to remember about testimonials:

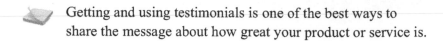 Getting and using testimonials is one of the best ways to share the message about how great your product or service is.

The best way to get testimonials is to ask for them, plain and simple.

Results-based testimonials speak to the *quality* of the product or service you provide.

Customer-service-based testimonials are extremely effective at helping to increase prospective customers' comfort level when considering doing business with your company.

To be credible, a testimonial must include the customer's full name, company name or town.

Use the testimonials in your print advertising, on your Web site, and in your newsletters.

Chapter Nine:
Benefits of Regular
Contact—
and Your Secret
Weapon!

A quick word of warning! This chapter contains phenomenal marketing information on how to grow your business and boost your profits with a monthly customer newsletter. This is the area of marketing that I am best known for. In fact, I'm known internationally as The Newsletter Guru. My opinions and recommendations are both strong and on solid ground, but you should also know that I'm going to challenge you throughout to avoid being what I call a newsletter pansy! For the good of your business, I encourage you not to take offense and read on.

Keep in Touch

You must stay in touch with your customers in order to build longevity and loyalty. It's estimated that 10 percent of your customers forget about you every month unless they hear from you! Yikes! If that doesn't shake you up, nothing will.

As any business owner knows, the highest producing sales representatives are always on the lookout for reasons to get in front of their customers, and, as we saw in a previous chapter, you have to remind customers about opportunities like your referral program. After you remind them, it's wise to tell them one or two more times, and probably once more after that.

Even your best customers need a little prodding now and then in order to buy from you again, and most prospects need several "touches" before they'll buy from you the first time. Many entrepreneurs will tell you that prospects need to hear from you seven to ten times before they convert from prospects to customers. Every "no" puts you one step closer to a "yes."

Even customers who love your product or service, have been the recipient of your over-the-top customer service, and have written glowing and powerful testimonials about you, need to be regularly reminded that you're there. That's called building top-of-mind awareness.

It's really simple—regular customer contact increases adhesion and keeps your customers sticking like glue for life.

The good news is, it's very easy to stay in touch with your customers.

Your Secret Weapon: The Magical Glue of a Monthly Newsletter

I'd like to share what Bill Glazer had to say about newsletters (and specifically about my book, *The Magic of Newsletter Marketing—The Secret to More Profits and Customers for Life*): "Who should be sending out newsletters to their customers/clients/patients/prospects? The answer is everybody!!! That's right; there is not a business on the planet that couldn't benefit BIG TIME with a monthly company newsletter. There is no better way to develop a relationship with people than sending out a properly written newsletter, and Jim Palmer is the go-to guy to help you get that done." Glazer knows the importance of good glue.

Sticky Note:
Newsletter publishing is like changing the oil in your car. There's no immediate gratification, but it keeps your car in good shape and running longer.

A monthly customer newsletter helps you stay top-of-mind with your current customers. Your newsletter arrives, and instantly your customers are thinking about you. After receiving your newsletter on a consistent basis, your customers actually begin to look forward to receiving it—it's a welcome friend—and they are curious to see what tips and stories you are sharing with them in the newest issue.

As we saw earlier in the book, there's a proliferation of advertising that makes it very difficult for your message to stand out, and that's exactly why a monthly custom newsletter program like my No Hassle Newsletter (www.NoHassleNewsletters.com) program works—it's *not* advertising!

The best and most successful newsletter programs provide information that has value to your customers. They're not overly promotional. While they may contain information about a special offer, include the latest winner in your referral contest (complete with photo and the value of the prize), and share your latest great testimonial (with full name, company, and results-oriented statement, of course), your newsletter must contain content that your customers find useful and entertaining.

A properly written customer newsletter is a marketing secret weapon.

Done correctly, friendly customer newsletters:

- keep your name and company in front of your customers on a regular basis.
- Newsletters provide valuable information that your customers not only appreciate but actually look forward to receiving.
- They provide the perfect vehicle to tell your customers about a new product, service, or offering.
- Newsletters also give you the forum to present more personal information about your company and staff. Customers can get to know you better, and the trust builds.

Remember, one of Zig Ziglar's five hurdles to closing a sale is "no trust." Newsletters can help you overcome that.

- Plus, when they show up monthly, they are perceived as having a high value like magazines.

Dollar for dollar, newsletters are the most effective marketing tool available. Plus, customers who read your newsletter are usually in a good position to do business with you again, and to recommend your product or service to others. And that's where your new business comes from!

This is what I call "the magic of newsletter marketing!"

As I mentioned, newsletters are not perceived in the same manner as are postcards, fliers, or other forms of direct mail marketing. When people receive these or anything else that has a sales and marketing feel to it, their guard goes up, and they think, "Uh-oh. What are they trying to sell me?"

Newsletters work well because they tend to be read as informational, making them more welcome when they are received. As such, they have higher readership than other forms of advertising. People also tend to be more receptive to what you have to say in your newsletter, because newsletters aren't meant to be sales tools. Rather, they are designed to be a resource.

Marketing genius Dan Kennedy put it this way: "People are conditioned to be less resistant to reading information such as articles than they are advertising." Because people are conditioned to be less resistant to reading information, which is exactly what a newsletter should be, most people read a newsletter with their guard down. This is a HUGE marketing advantage. When your customers' guards are down, they are open and receptive to what you have to say!

A customer newsletter is the strongest marketing and business-building tool available—bar none.

Newsletters open doors.

According to Kennedy, it's important to build a strong "fence" around your customers to keep them close. Regular contact with your customers is one of the best ways to build and maintain a strong fence that keeps your customers in. In his book, *NO B.S. Direct Marketing*, Kennedy writes, "My single biggest recommendation is the use of a monthly customer newsletter. Nothing, and I mean nothing, maintains your fence better."

7 Secrets of Successful Newsletter Marketing

Let me share 7 secrets with you about newsletter marketing that will bring you success.

#1: Newsletters help you keep customers.

As we saw in the first chapter of *Stick Like Glue*, it's far more costly to acquire new customers than it is to retain your existing ones. Remember the leaky bucket? A good newsletter program helps you plug the leaks by creating relationships with your customers. When you share information in your newsletter, you build trust and establish rapport. When you share *valuable* information, your customers will actually look forward to receiving your newsletter. Plus it helps you stay top-of-mind with them. As soon as they receive it, they're thinking about you and your company. Issue after issue, you build stronger relationships with your customers.

#2: Newsletters help you get new customers.

Good, informative articles give your newsletter what marketing pros call "pass-along" value. When a customer passes along one of your newsletters to a friend, relative, or colleague, you get a referral. Your customers don't simply hand over your newsletter. They'll hand it over with a statement like, "Charlie, you have got to read this. I read this article and know it will help you as well. And XYZ Company is great. I deal with them all the time."

People read newsletters as publications, not as marketing pieces, so they're more receptive to the information they contain…including information about your company and what you offer. When faced with blatant marketing materials like brochures and sales literature, most readers work to block the information, because we're all too inundated with advertisements every day. But when newsletters offer articles and valuable information, they're more likely to be read, remembered, and passed along.

Send newsletters to all of your customers, and I do mean all of them. Don't be selective and stingy, sending only to those who spend a specified amount with you. You never know when a small customer is on the verge of turning into a big one! Send your newsletters to all of your prospects and to anyone who's requested information about your company as well. Remember, it takes seven to ten "touches" to convert a prospect into a paying customer.

Have your sales staff hand out your current issue when making calls, and integrate the newsletter into the sales process. They should point out appropriate articles or new product offerings.

Provide your newsletters to your local Chamber of Commerce and have them available for community events. You certainly want to have them with you at trade shows and exhibitions, and you can also include them with checks when mailing payments to you vendors. Be certain that your Web site has a link to both your current edition as well as an archive of all past editions.

#3: Newsletters help build credibility.

When people read your brochure, they read it as advertising and are naturally resistant to the message. However, when they read your newsletter, they read it like a publication, and the message gets through. You can share tips and stories about how others benefited from your product or service. Include statistics and testimonials. They help build credibility.

#4: Newsletters help you stand out from your competition.

You differentiate yourself with a monthly newsletter, because you're staying in regular contact with your customers and providing them with valuable information. In most cases, your competitors are not doing that. Newsletters work to keep customers glued to you. They keep them fenced in and your competitors out.

#5: Newsletters are the perfect way to show that you're an expert in your field.

By sharing useful articles with your customers about your industry, you can set yourself apart as the expert. After all, you are. While your newsletter recipients might not need your product or service when they receive the newsletter, you're continually planting the seed that you are the perfect person to turn to when they do. People want to do business with someone they trust, and you become that person by sharing your expertise.

#6: Newsletters help you build your brand.

Branding is all about creating recognition and awareness of who you are and what you offer. Repetition is a requirement for brand building. Think of that famous Nike logo that's referred to as a swoosh. I don't have to show it to you, and I probably didn't have to tell you the company's name. You've seen it so many times that it's immediately recognizable. In fact, the company doesn't even have to use its name on athletic shoes and apparel.

The logo now says it all. That's the importance of consistency and repetition in brand building.

Marketing research varies on how often you need to have regular contact with customers in order to make your brand stick. Some suggest between seven and nine contacts in eighteen months. Others suggest monthly contact, and that's what I believe. My personal research and experience show that the best results come from a *monthly* customer newsletter. It shows up like clockwork like any other magazine or subscription, and that adds to its perceived value. When your newsletter arrives in customers' mailboxes at the same time each month, it increases its importance and helps build your brand.

#7: Newsletters have a longer shelf life than other forms of marketing.

Newsletters that provide useful information aren't quickly discarded. I know people who literally sort their mail over their trash cans. Anything that looks like advertising goes right in without ever being opened. That's not the fate of newsletters, because they contain valuable and entertaining information.

They're easy to take anywhere—to the office, home, on a plane, to kids' soccer games—everywhere and anywhere. Besides having a long shelf life with the original recipient, they're often passed on to other colleagues, business associates, friends, and neighbors. The secondary recipients then tend to take them anywhere and everywhere. All that time, your brand is getting out there. More people are learning about what you offer and its value. This is one of the huge benefits of newsletter marketing.

The Trump Card: Consistency

Regular and frequent contact is an absolute must to both strengthen your glue and to get results from your newsletter program.

Newsletters are not a quick fix. I always tell customers that it takes between six and nine months to see positive results from a newsletter program. You cannot expect to transform your business overnight by sending a single newsletter. Don't give up after sending only two or three issues. I call those people "newsletter pansies," and you don't want to fall into that category.

Consistency is the most important factor in successful newsletter marketing. In fact, I regularly tell audiences that a plain-looking, two-page, black and white newsletter mailed like clockwork every month will far outperform a splashy, full-color newsletter that's mailed quarterly.

Consistency trumps all else.

I'll share a story about how consistency really paid off…to the tune of closing a $150,000 sale. When I was in the franchise business, every prospective franchisee who read one of our franchise opportunity ads and called our office then received our brochure and went into our normal franchise-marketing funnel. However, I also added their names to our mailing list so that they started receiving our monthly newsletter as well.

By the way, the normal sales cycle on a franchise is three to six months. During that time, most candidates will generally decide to either move forward or pass on the opportunity and simply disappear.

I remember one man who was initially very interested. He came out for a visit, and we even did some preliminary site work. It began to look like the sale was going somewhere, and then he just disappeared. After almost nine months, he re-contacted our company, and we ended up opening a franchise for him. When he came in for his initial two-week training prior to opening his store, I remember meeting with him, and I asked him why it took almost two years to get to this point. He said, "Jim, I really wanted to buy into the franchise, but initially I just was not comfortable with the stability, so I held off." I said, "That's completely understandable, but something must have changed your mind. What was it?"

As it turned out, this guy was reading our newsletter month after month. Let me tell you a little about this newsletter. On the front cover, I featured what I called the Score Card, which listed the number of stores open, the number of stores in progress, and the total number of stores. Month after month, the total number of stores was increasing. In addition, he was reading articles about successful franchisees who were exceeding their sales goals, and about some franchisees who were opening their second and third locations. He then told me that, after a while, he realized his worry about stability was unfounded, and he told me he "wanted to be part of this success train!"

In large part, our monthly newsletter actually sealed the deal for him. I also remember that some directors in the company thought the monthly newsletter was a big waste of time and resources, but in this case, it was the newsletter that sold a $150,000 franchise.

Don't be a newsletter pansy. You never know when a prospect may be ready to convert and write you a big check. If this guy had only received two or three editions, we never would have made that sale.

Based on my nearly thirty years' experience in marketing and growing businesses with newsletters, both for my previous employers and now for my hundreds of clients and customers in seven different countries, I am 100 percent confident that if you follow my advice and suggestions and are not a newsletter pansy, you will see more profits and customers for life in your business—no matter what business you are in!

My belief in friendly customer newsletters as an amazing—almost magical—marketing tool is so strong that, in 2001, when I decided to go into business for myself, I knew that newsletters would be my main offering. And what a ride it's been!

My belief in friendly customer newsletters is so strong that I believe anyone who doesn't mail a monthly newsletter to customers is simply being a newsletter pansy. There is simply too much empirical evidence and data that prove my case.

It's a fact that customer newsletters help businesses succeed. And the best and most effective way to grow your business, boost your profits, and get more customers for life is to *mail monthly.* Anything less frequent than monthly means that you are simply being a newsletter pansy!

Learn more secrets on how to grow your business with a newsletter by getting a copy of my book, *The Magic of Newsletter Marketing—The Secret to More Profits and Customers for Life* at www.NewsletterPublishingMagic.com.

Newsletter Content

It doesn't take any more work to produce a great newsletter than a mediocre one, so don't be a newsletter pansy—create a great one.

One of the keys to a great newsletter is content, and in order to provide great content, you need to do a little planning. You need to determine what you want to achieve with your newsletter. Addressing your customers' needs and interests will put you on the right path to getting what you want.

When I started writing newsletters years ago, I always envisioned that I was having a conversation with the reader. I still do. That's what makes a newsletter interesting, entertaining, and valuable. It's the perfect vehicle for you to have a personal conversation with hundreds or thousands of your customers at the same time. Here are the questions you need to answer as part of your planning:

Who will read the newsletter? A successful newsletter is *not* about you or what you want to write about. It's about the readers and what they want to read about!

Envision your perfect target customer when deciding what to include in your newsletter. Think about the typical age, gender, or specific demographic that fits your ideal customer. You want your newsletter to be a conversation with this person. Don't try to think about all of your customers and prospects when writing your newsletter. Instead, think about one single person and write your newsletter in a friendly and conversational tone. That's exactly the point of your monthly newsletter in the first place—to have a conversation with your reader.

What problems do my customers have? What do they want to know about? Your newsletter will only be great if it's filled with articles and information that your customers want to read. If it's filled with a lot of self-promotional advertising, your customers are going to perceive it as just another marketing piece. They won't be looking forward to it each month and may toss it right in the trash at mail-sorting time.

On the other hand, if it's informative, interesting, and entertaining, your customers will actually look forward to receiving it every month. My recommended ratio is 50/50—half of it focused on your company, products, and services (work stuff), and the other half on articles and stories that meet the "informative, interesting, and entertaining" criteria (what I call "other stuff").

Typically, this half doesn't have anything to do with your business at all, but it's what makes your newsletter successful.

Sticky Note:
Subscribe to Success Advantage, and 90% of your newsletter (including ALL of the "other stuff") will be done for you. Check out www.TheNewsletterGuru.com/solutions.

The work stuff that you include is not simply advertising. Think about the questions you hear most often from your customers. They're asking because it's information they want. Include that information as part of the work stuff in your monthly newsletter. Don't make it specifically about your business. Make it about information that your customers want to know.

Also, tell your customers what *else* you do. Remember—one of the ways to grow your business and increase your profitability is to sell more to your existing customers. Be certain your customers know about all of your products and services by mentioning them in your monthly newsletter.

You can also tell them what's new in your company. If you've got a new product launch, put it in your newsletter. But don't just tell about it. Think about how your new product will benefit your customers. That's what you want to address in your newsletter. Don't forget about everyone's favorite station: WII-FM (What's In It for Me?).

What is your newsletter name and tagline? Your newsletter masthead is the major graphic element on the front. It should identify your company and may even indicate that your company presents the newsletter. However, in most cases, I recommend that your newsletter title should not be your company name.

Your tagline is the subtitle and should appear at the bottom of the masthead. It works in conjunction with the title and should explain the benefit of reading your newsletter. For example, a salon may offer a newsletter titled "Personal Style" with the tagline "Information and tips on hair, skin, nails, and looking & feeling great."

What should be in every issue? In addition to consistent delivery, you want to maintain a consistent presentation of the information that's included in your newsletter.

First, every issue will obviously have a main article for the front page. You'll want to use work stuff, but it must be presented in a way that does not appear to be selling anything.

A great idea is to tell about another customer's success story with your product or service. Readers will quickly be able to envision themselves in the same situation.

Other ideas for interesting work stuff include new customer welcomes, customer and employee profiles, and results of surveys you may have taken.

Next, your back page is an important piece of real estate in your newsletter. It's typically opposite the mailing panel, and is nearly always read. In fact, it's probably second only to your front page for exposure and readability. Special offers, product launches, or a personal monthly message are great choices for this location.

When thinking about the "other stuff" that goes into your newsletter, keep in mind that customers love to learn new things; they love stories; they love to learn about things that are better or free; and everyone loves humor. If it sounds too daunting to develop this content every month (shameless plug alert), subscribe to Success Advantage. We'll provide you with a ton of content from which you can pick and choose, to include as the "other stuff" in your newsletter.

Sticky Note:
For more in-depth information about creating a successful
monthly newsletter, check out my first book,
The Magic of Newsletter Marketing—The Secret to More
Profits and Customers for Life
at www.NewsletterPublishingMagic.com.

Writing Copy

One of the most important things to keep in mind when writing your work stuff content is that it must be engaging and interesting, or it isn't going to be read. I know that a lot of people can be intimidated when it comes to sitting down and writing, and there's an easy way to get over that hurdle.

Simply envision yourself having a conversation with your customer. You probably have no hesitation picking up the phone and calling your customers, right? Don't let your articles be any different. Write the same way you talk. That's what keeps people reading them. Use the same words that you'd use in a conversation. Don't use a lot of jargon or acronyms in excess. Use common words, simple sentences, and short paragraphs.

Let your personality shine through when writing your newsletter. Remember, you're building a relationship with your customers. They buy from someone they know, not a company. Let them get to know you.

Use a lot of bullet points, and even a Q &A section in your articles.

Use humor. If you inject humor into conversations with your customers, there's no reason not to include it in your newsletter articles.

Keep it short too. Great newsletters are read in less than ten minutes. Don't be boring, and don't mention things your customers have no interest in. You may be really proud about an award your company just won, but unless it's really meaningful to your customers, don't drone on about it. A simple statement will suffice.

Write in your own words. Don't plagiarize. The Internet has made it really easy to cut and paste information. The problem with that is very simple: It is illegal. If you want to use a sentence or two, you must attribute it to the original author. If you want to use more, get permission, preferably in writing. There are article banks and sites from which you can draw content, but you must abide by their conditions in order to legally use the material.

The Magic AIDA Formula

AIDA is the acronym for "attention, interest, data (or desire), and action." It works magic when you apply it to newsletter writing.

First you have to grab your reader's **attention**. You've got a powerful message to deliver, but it won't go anywhere unless you draw some attention to it.

Pique interest when creating your article headlines. Entice the reader to think, "I have to read this. I don't want to miss it!" In my earliest newsletter days, when I was writing for the bike shop, I used the headline "The Secret to Riding Four Hours Instead of Forty Minutes." The article was about padded bike shorts, and trust me—that headline drew a lot more attention than "Bike Shorts: $20."

I'll share three quick tips about classic headlines. The first one uses the word "How" as the lead. "How a 40-Year-Old Can Retire in 15 Years." "How the Next 90 Days Can Change Your Life." The formula is: How + Subject (who the article is targeted to) + Benefit.

The second classic headline is "If You / You Can." For example, "If You Are a Safe Driver, You Can Save 20% on Your Car Insurance." It's: If You + Requirement + Benefit. "If You Can Read This Section, You Can Write Great Headlines."

The third classic headline is a number, followed by an achievement. "Ten Ways to Keep Your Customers Coming Back." "Four Easy Ways to Feel Younger." The more impressive the number, the better, but you have to back it up. Don't promise ten and deliver nine!

The next part of the AIDA magic is **interest**. You've grabbed them with your headline, and now you have to draw them into the article.

Telling a story is a great way to create interest, but there's one caveat to your storytelling. Your reader must be able to identify with the subject of your story. They'll relate to it and keep reading if the story is about someone like them.

You also want your story to generate some emotion. Essentially, people buy for two reasons—to run away from pain or to run toward gain. Emotion drives either of those points home and facilitates the buying decision. Tell a story that relates to your reader, generates some emotion, and provides the solution(s) that the article title suggested, and you've developed interest.

Data or **desire** is the "D" in the AIDA acronym. Once you drive the point home with emotion, you've got to make your case with logic. A lot of people will buy on an emotional level, but the rest of them need a more scientific, proven reason. That's were data comes in. Back up your claims with logic and data.

Testimonials are one way to do that. You get your prospect nodding in agreement as he reads an article about someone like him; he's emotionally drawn to your solution, but…oops…not quite enough to act. Seal the deal by providing a testimonial. Tell him about someone just like him who had success with your product.

Statistics are another way to shore up your argument. Be credible and cite your sources. That creates the same authority and trustworthiness as identifying your testimonial providers with full name and company. Your reader probably won't double-check it, but they know they can if they want to. It's more convincing.

Finally, the last part of AIDA is **action**. You've gotten their attention, raised interest, supported your claims with data and built desire, but there's still one critical step. You don't make the sale unless you ask.

Don't let your story end without telling your reader exactly what you want them to do. Don't presume your reader will know, and don't be too timid to ask. Tell them exactly what you want, and lead them there step-by-step. Bill Glazer has suggested that, for many of us, the target customer is Homer Simpson. If you think about Homer when writing your action steps, it enables you to write it simplistically and clearly. Don't assume your customer is going to connect all the dots. You've got to invite them to do it, and then show them how.

Issue after issue, your newsletter reinforces your relationship with your customers. It makes your fence stronger. It also gives you a way to tell current customers about products and services you provide that they may not know about.

So there you have it—I simply can't say it any more clearly!

Publishing a monthly customer newsletter is smart. Not doing so, no matter what business you're in, is simply being a newsletter pansy.

What you do with the information I've shared about newsletter marketing is entirely your decision. Only you can take action to get and keep more customers now. Only you can take action to build healthier, stronger relationships with your customers, clients, and prospects. Only you can begin to boost your profits by doing more repeat and referral business with your current customers! I'll conclude this section with a challenge.

I challenge you to start or restart your monthly customer newsletter now, and to continue it every month. Now go do it, and don't be a newsletter pansy!

To learn everything there is to know about crafting and producing easy and effective customer newsletters so that you remain in your customers' top-of-mind awareness, I highly recommend my book (hey, a good book is a good book!), *The Magic of Newsletter Marketing: The Secret to More Profits and Customers for Life.*

Learn more at www.NewsletterPublishingMagic.com.

> *Sticky Note:*
> **People like to do business with other people, not with "companies." Sending newsletters allows you to put a face on your business and lets your customers get to know the people rather than the company.**

More Ideas for Keeping in Touch

Sending hand-written **thank-you notes** is another great way to keep in touch with your customers and keep them sticking. Never underestimate the power of a hand-written thank-you note! It's easy, quick, and can be more powerful than your most finely executed marketing campaign.

Social scientist Randy Garner wanted to test the power of a hand-written note in improving response rates for a mailed survey. One group received a hand-written note on a sticky note attached to the cover letter of the survey; a second group received a hand-written note on the cover letter itself; and the third group received only the cover letter and survey. The results? Of the recipients who received the cover letter with the sticky note, 75% of them completed and returned the survey, compared to 48% who received the hand-written note on the cover letter, and 36% who did not receive any sort of hand-written note. (From *Yes! 50 Scientifically Proven Ways to Be Persuasive.*)

As you can see, the effort to hand-write a note (and take an extra step to attach it on a small sticky paper), had the greatest impact.

When you see an article or some bit of information that your customer might find interesting, take a minute to jot a note and send it to him or her. Maybe it's about the company or industry. Think you're too time-strapped to handle the task? You could take ten minutes each day to jot a few notes. It truly won't take any more time than that. Never ever underestimate the power of a personal and hand-written note!

Be sure to use personalization. There's power in personalization. Study after study proves it. As Dale Carnegie noted long ago in *How to Win Friends and Influence People*, using a person's name makes you more likeable to them. Carnegie said, "Remember that a person's name is to them the sweetest and most important sound in any language." That hasn't changed one iota. Be sure to take advantage of it! You're more apt to be able to persuade people who like you than those who don't!

But using a customer's name goes far beyond persuasion and getting them to buy. It makes people happy. Making your customers happy is the only way to make them stick.

Use your customers' names when you speak with them and in all your communications. Remember in my previous example how I asked for Tom's name? I'm certain that helped diffuse the situation.

Direct mail studies have shown that response rates improve by almost 50 percent simply by personalizing it. "Dear Mr. Jones" gets a far better response than "Dear Friend." Use the data you've collected about your customers to the fullest extent possible. Even if you've only got their names.

Sticky Note:
According to a study by Romano and Broudy, personalized direct mail garners a 44% response rate increase over the generic "Dear Friend" counterpart.

Social media is another great way to build relationships with customers and prospects. Sites like Facebook®, Twitter®, and LinkedIn® are ideal and easy ways to keep friendly reminders about your company in front of your customers.

You can reach out to your customers on these sites every day if you'd like. In a few minutes per day, you can share your message and help people get to know you better.

However, it's important that you have something worthwhile to share! I started with a regular Facebook® profile page, and when I reached 5000 friends (the maximum allowed by Facebook®), I then created my fan page. I post a combination of inspiring and motivational quotes, entrepreneurial success tips, various marketing strategies, newsletter critiques, videos, and pictures. All are strategically designed to help people get to know me better—to know what I stand for and what value I can bring to their business. I post similar information to my Twitter® page, although with Twitter® you are limited to 140 characters per post.

I invite you to connect with me on my Facebook® fan page. Go to www.Facebook.com/TheNewsletterGuru. You can also follow me on Twitter® by going to www.Twitter.com/NewsletterGuru. You can find me at LinkedIn® by searching "Jim Palmer," and you can also check out my videos at www.NewsletterGuru.TV.

I also use social sites to share information about marketing tips as I discover them, often in real time, which is an exciting part of social media. Sometimes I'll share a link to a great article, or upload a short video explaining something that I feel has value to grow visitors' businesses. Videos are very powerful, because people get to see and hear you, your mannerisms, voice inflection, and more. These sites are very effective tools for building what I call the "know, like, and trust" factor with my clients.

Sticking Points:

Here's the recap of the important points to remember about regular customer contact and monthly customer newsletter programs:

 It's estimated that 10 percent of your customers forget about you every month unless they hear from you!

 Good sales reps *look* for reasons to get in front of customers. Regular contact keeps you top-of-mind.

 A monthly newsletter helps to build and maintain a strong fence around your customers to keep them in.

 Newsletters have incredible pass-along value, and are a great way to get referrals and brand-new customers.

 Newsletters have perceived value like magazines. Readers are much more open to reading and remembering them.

 Consistency trumps everything else! Your newsletter gains perceived value when it goes out like clockwork.

 Picture your perfect customer and write your newsletter to that individual. Write conversationally and in a friendly tone!

 Remember the AIDA formula: Attention, Interest, Data/Desire, and finally Action. Be specific with your call to action. Tell your readers exactly what you want them to do.

 Stay in touch with your customers. Newsletters, hand-written notes, and social media sites are the perfect vehicles to do so.

Chapter Ten:
Up the Ante

Follow the Money

Remember the movie *Jerry Maguire*? The Cuba Gooding Jr. character had Jerry, played by Tom Cruise, keep shouting, "Show me the money!" A variation of this is "Follow the Money!" Successful entrepreneurs know the importance of following the money. When their customers ask for something, these entrepreneurs find a way to supply their customers with whatever they want. That's what following the money is all about—go where the money leads. After all, you're in business to make a profit.

Granted, there are some who keep a narrow focus on what they're willing to provide and don't stray off the original path they put themselves on when they went into business in the first place. Their mindset is "I sell widgets, and that's what I know and love, so I'm sticking to widgets. If my customers want thing-a-ma-jigs to go with their widgets, well, they'll have to find them someplace else. I'm in the widget business."

I won't say there's anything *completely* wrong with this approach. If it makes the widget guy happy, that's his choice. But I do know this—he's missing a golden opportunity to grow his business and make more money. What's more, if his competitor decides to sell thing-a-ma-jigs in addition to widgets, this widget-only guy is setting himself up to lose customers and profits. And remember, he's not simply losing a sale; he'll be losing the lifetime value of those thing-a-ma-jig-loving customers! If you narrow your focus, I guarantee you're limiting your opportunities, and your bank deposit will be smaller at month's end.

Successful businesses continue to expand their offerings. They continue to follow the money.

This may be a good time to briefly describe the difference between an entrepreneur and a business owner.

Most **business owners** focus on their core businesses and think that continued growth will come from selling more of what they offer. For example, if you're a jewelry store owner, your approach toward growth is selling more jewelry or perhaps opening a second location. In other words, it's simply more of what your current business is.

Conversely, an **entrepreneur** looks for opportunities to create more value so that they can create more wealth. Part of this mindset is having an open mind to selling new products or services to your current customers, or even a new way to distribute your goods and services.

One individual is focused on selling more ___ (fill in the blank), and the other is focused on creating more wealth by delivering more value to customers.

Since it's easiest to sell to your top customers—the hyper-responsive ones—that should be your focus as you follow the money.

I strongly encourage every entrepreneur to become intimately familiar with his or her customer list. To begin with, you should not only identify your top 20 percent, you should also segment your list by identifying the top 10 percent, top 5 percent, and even your top 2 percent.

Here's why. Your top 2 to 5 percent of customers are not your typical customer. They should receive different marketing messages and even different offers than the typical customer. If your goal is to sell as much as possible and achieve the highest possible profits (and that's a worthy goal), this can be made much easier by selling to your repeat customers in unique and different ways.

Let me give you just one example. If one of your customers in the top 2 percent regularly purchases the best of what you sell and upgrades to the best service package you offer, does it make sense to send him or her a mailer with a coupon for 10 percent off their next purchase? I think not. Conversely, it would be inappropriate to send your average customer a special offer for your top-of-the-line product complete with your platinum level service agreement. You can unquestionably make more money by focusing your marketing and offers to the right targeted list of customers.

How can you figure out what else your customers might be interested in? For starters, keep your eyes and ears open. Many of the products and services I now offer were created as a direct result of listening to what my customers' pain-points were. Let me illustrate this by giving you a brief history of No Hassle Newsletters.

When I first created this program, I started by offering some newsletter articles that my customers could use in their company newsletters. I know from experience that one of the biggest reasons that more companies don't mail a monthly newsletter is that they never know what to include. I relived them of this "pain" by providing them some great articles and content. When some of my customers told me they loved it, I then branded it my Customer-Loving™ content.

Next, some customers told me they loved the content but sometimes struggled with newsletter design. So I created easy-to-use and ready-to-go newsletter templates. As I continued to expand the benefits of this program, I also raised my price.

The next big upgrade came when my company was exhibiting at a national marketing event. One of my current customers came up and said that he loves my content and newsletter templates but he struggles getting his newsletter printed and mailed. In less than thirty days, I unveiled The Newsletter Guru's Concierge Print and Mail on Demand service.

Are you starting to see a pattern? When I started out, I had no idea that I would be in the printing business, but by keeping my eyes and ears open, and being flexible to let my business continuously evolve, I've continued to grow and create more value and, in turn, create a more profitable business.

Did all of this take some work and research on my part? You bet it did, but it was an obvious way to grow my business.

Never being one to coast too long, I then created and launched my second customer-relationship and business-building tool: Newsletter Postcards (www.NewsletterPostcards.com). This is a large, full-color postcard with the familiar look and feel of a customer newsletter. Still keeping my ears open and listening to my customers, I next created The Newsletter Guru's StandOUT E-zine program. (If you'd like to see what a StandOUT E-zine looks like go to www.JimsNewsletter.com.) My most current example of listening to what my customers want is my mastermind and coaching group. Masterminding is without a doubt one of the best ways to grow a business, and some entrepreneurs were also inquiring about having me coach them in their business. So guess what I did? I developed Jim Palmer's Outrageous Mastermind/Coaching group. You can learn more about this opportunity at www.TheNewsletterGuru.com.

The lesson you should take from this brief business history lesson is this: If you put blinders on (like the guy selling only widgets), you will be limited as to how much you can realistically grow your business. However, if you remove the blinders, think like an entrepreneur, and keep your eyes and ears open to what your customers are asking for—and if you are prepared to give it to them—there is no limit as to how much you can increase your business!

If you're not exactly sure which products or services can be profitably added to your arsenal, here's a very easy way to find out: Ask! Go back to your customer list and focus on your top customers. Create a survey to bounce your ideas off them, and measure the responses. It can be as easy as listing your ideas with a one to ten scale, and have them rate how likely (or unlikely) they'd be to buy or use it.

Even if you don't have expansion ideas to present in the form of a survey, the solution to finding out what else your customers might be interested in is the same: Ask! Every time you speak with a customer, you can end the conversation with a very friendly request for information from them. "So, Mr. Jones, it's been a pleasure serving you. May I ask what you like about doing business with ABC Company?" Follow that up with "And is there anything we don't offer that you'd like to see in the future?"

When you hear similar requests from different customers, you'll know you're on to something, and the path for you to follow the money begins to open up. Following the money grows your business and increases your profits.

Would You Like Fries with That?

How many times in your life have you heard that question? That ubiquitous fast food restaurant probably perfected the art of up-selling with that simple question. Does it work? Of course it does! How many times have you heard that question and answered "yes"? You may not have been thinking about fries when you placed your order, but that question puts the idea in your head. This fast food company didn't make all their profits on the "billions and billions" sold. Along with those "billions and billions" went billions of orders of fries too!

Selling more to your customers is more profitable than getting new customers, but in order to sell more, your customers have to know what else you offer. You have to tell them. Up-sell, up-sell, up-sell. It's been a few pages, so let me share another story from my bike shops days!

Some of you reading this book may be too young to remember, but we didn't always have computers. In the old days, we used to have to write up every sale on a carbonless receipt. Well, one of the things I did to increase profits was conduct regular contests to see which employee could fill up the most lines on the receipt with add-on accessories. I figured it this way. The customers already said yes to a new bike, perhaps costing $250, so how hard would it be for them to say yes to some accessories that would make their new purchases more enjoyable?

This strategy worked very well, but I also noticed that some customers will only say yes so many times, even if it's something they want. So the next thing I did was to create accessory packages. Following the strategies made popular by Sears® and Radio Shack®, I created a good, better, and best packages, with each one containing highly popular accessories that the average customer was saying yes to. By creating the special accessory packages, our customers only had to say yes one time after saying yes to the initial purchase of the bike—only this one yes was very profitable!

This strategy proved very effective at increasing both the average sale and our gross profit. Think about it. What items can you bundle in your business to make it easy to add some additional profit to each sale?

There are many ways to get the message out there about your other products and services, but the easiest way is to tell…and then ask. Tell them what you have available that might further benefit them, then ask them if they would like the additional item(s). The question "Would you like fries with that?" is the perfect example. It lets the customer know there's another product to consider, and asks for the sale at the same time.

Increasing the value of the transaction grows your business, not only with that single transaction but with the lifetime value as well! Up-selling is a no-brainer idea. If you're not up-selling, I guarantee you're leaving money on the table. Easy money. In fact, you're ignoring the easiest money you can possibly make if you aren't up-selling to your customers.

Think about all of those entrepreneurs and companies that offer standard and deluxe packages. They start with the standard package and mention the upgrade just before the buyer is ready to sign. The buyer already sees value in the offering and has agreed to it. "But before we proceed, Mr. Jones, let me tell you about our deluxe package. You'll get everything we offer in the standard package along with benefits X, Y and Z, and it's only a few dollars more."

As a consumer, you've probably heard it hundreds of times. Think about the last time you bought a new car. You'd finally agreed to the price and terms and signed on the dotted line. Before you could drive away, you certainly heard about extended warranties, under-carriage protection, clear coat, etc., etc., etc. The sale person was doing his or her best to increase the value of the transaction. This scenario is a bit more complicated than "Would you like fries with that?" but the end result is the same.

> *Sticky Note:*
> If you aren't up-selling, you're leaving the easiest money you'll ever make on the table. Why walk away from it? Up-sell, up-sell, up-sell!

Cross-Selling

Not every product or service you offer builds on the one before it, but you've still got more you can offer to your customers. That's where cross-selling comes in.

Cross-selling doesn't necessarily increase the value of a particular transaction, but it does provide you with a means to sell more to your current customers. There are very few companies that sell just one thing, just one product or one service. They almost always sell a multitude of things or offer a number of various services, especially if they've been savvy about following the money.

When you get a new customer, you do so by way of a single transaction. While it's always a good thing to close a sale, be warned that you are far from bringing in a valued lifetime customer with a single transaction. Far from it. This single transaction is just the beginning of what you hope will be a long-term profitable relationship. But there's much work to do! Your customer is getting to know you, and with good glue, you're starting to build the foundation for the know, like, and trust factor. When you get them sticking like glue, they'll want to buy from you again and again. Your company will be the first one they think of when they want what you sell. However, you have to have something to offer them, especially if your initial offering isn't a consumable or if it is something that has a very long shelf life. This is especially critical during tough economic times.

Find out what else your customers want or need and sell it to them. Typically, your customers' ability to consume will outpace your ability to offer, so you should always be on the lookout for new opportunities; always be on the lookout for new paths and new ways to follow the money.

Sticky Note:
Your customers' desire to buy from you often outpaces your ability to sell. One of the easiest ways to find out what else your customer wants and needs is simply to ask!

Creating a full complement of products and services is only the first step. Next, you've got to tell your customers what else is available. This is one area that works particularly well for newsletters. Use your newsletter to tell your customers "what else." Most customers, even your best ones, have no idea about all the products and services you sell.

Remember that the best sales people are always looking for reasons to get in front of their clients. New products and services are great reasons to do just that. Again, it circles back to what we covered in the last chapter about maintaining regular contact with your customers.

If you choose to use your monthly customer newsletter to talk about your other products and services, be sure to do it in a way that isn't blatantly a sales pitch, or you are going to lose readership. You do not want your newsletter having a salesy or marketing feel to it. Remember, your content and messages must have value to your customers. They're still listening to that same old station: WII-FM (What's In It for Me?). When you talk about the other products you offer, I suggest doing so by way of success stories. Share how some of your customers are using or have used what you offer to their benefit. Your message should focus on how others benefited from using your company, and whenever possible, include a results-based testimonial.

Here's an example. I worked with an insurance company that offered a free initial consultation or audit. This is a fairly common practice, but, let's face it, most customers don't get too excited about this because they fear it is just an opportunity for the company to sell. So I helped this company take a far better and more creative approach by writing a success story article in their customer newsletter. Instead of running an article that described the audit process and its benefits with a generic headline like "ABC Insurance Offers Audits," the headline they used read, "Local Manufacturing Company Saves $23,000 in Premiums." with the subhead: "And Here's How They Did It."

I can assure you that every business owner who saw that headline read the article. No company is going to pass over the opportunity to save that kind of money on insurance! The article went on to describe exactly how the audit uncovered areas where this manufacturer was paying too much for insurance as well as areas where they were short on coverage. They also included a quote from the company president, mentioning how valuable the audit was. The majority of the article was about this company's success story with an ancillary product. It closed with a simple sentence: "To find out how you might also be able to benefit from an audit, contact us today." They were selling without selling.

Readers of this newsletter had their proverbial guards down, because they were reading information, not marketing literature. I'm certain there were plenty of other insurance customers who could see themselves in the same situation and started to wonder about their own insurance coverage. "Maybe I should give this insurance audit thing a try...."

Other Uses

In addition to keeping your eyes and ears open for the new products and services your customers might be interested in and new ways to sell them, keep them open for new and unusual ways in which your product is being used, and be ready to capitalize on that.

When Avon® first brought its Skin So Soft® product to market, it was a bath oil. Their target was women who wanted smoother skin, and that's how they marketed it. As it turned out, this product turned out to be fantastic for a number of other uses including removing adhesive residues, cleaning off paint, and also as a bug repellent.

While the original product designer may have been dismayed by these very incongruous alternative uses, the company's marketing department ultimately seized the opportunity. There aren't a lot of men looking for bath oil for themselves, but the other uses for this product turned out to be extremely attractive to them. The company doubled their target audience!

Not only was the company not offended by the fact that their product was being used as an insect repellent rather than as a bath oil, they embraced it. Today, they offer four different products as insect repellents that are spinoffs from the original bath oil they created. Very simply, they followed the money.

In addition to finding other uses, you should be looking for ways that your customers can use more of the product you offer. Think about shampoo. Have you ever read the instructions on the bottle? "Lather, rinse, repeat." REPEAT! Does anyone really need to repeat the process in order to get clean hair? In all likelihood, no. However, that one little word creates the potential for doubling sales. It gets people to use more of the product.

Joint Ventures—Co-Promotions

While you're following the money, you will probably come to realize that a joint venture or co-promotion also makes great sense. First things first. You have to have some sort of relationship with your JV partner. That relationship can be as simple as geographic location and proximity. For example, the pizza shop and the dry cleaner located in the same strip mall can offer each other's coupons. They're not competing with each other, so why not share customers? Most people shop within a five-mile radius of their homes, so why not promote each other's business and take advantage of the fact that most customers support the closest vendors?

Obviously, you're not going to promote your competition. The pizza shop located next to the dry cleaner isn't going to distribute coupons for the pizza shop one mile down the road, but there's no reason not to promote neighboring, non-competitive businesses...provided they're worthwhile. By that I mean that they offer solid customer service and stand behind their product as solidly as you stand behind yours.

Sticky Note:

Successful joint ventures provide win-win situations for both parties. They're a great way to expand your customer base by sharing customers with neighboring businesses or from parallel industries.

I wouldn't recommend entering into any sort of joint venture with a company with which *you* would not do business. If you can honestly say you'd use them, go ahead and suggest a JV. If your neighboring businesses aren't very customer centric, you may want to think twice about it.

In order for a JV to work, it must be a win-win for both companies. You must be able to promote each other's customer bases. In the example above, there's an excellent chance that folks who eat pizza also need dry cleaning on occasion, and vice versa. As long as the pizza man and the dry cleaner offer similar levels of customer service, it's a win-win for them.

Geographic proximity is the easiest joint venture approach, but you don't have to stop there. Think outside the box, as the popular saying goes. Ask yourself what else your customers buy that is parallel to what you offer, and explore the JV opportunities that can springboard from that.

For example, the jeweler will quickly expand his services to include jewelry repair and jewelry cleaning, in addition to retail sales. After all, anyone who buys a piece of jewelry is going to need it cleaned and perhaps repaired at some point. Those are obvious. Let's think about what's less obvious, but certainly viable.

Our jeweler begins thinking about the places his patrons go while wearing the jewelry they've purchased from him. Ah, they often go to the theatre! With that in mind, he can contact the local theatre and suggest a JV. Maybe he gives out discount theatre coupons with jewelry purchases, and the theatre owner reciprocates. In both cases, it can be a win-win situation, and both entrepreneurs may end up with new parallel customers.

By following the money, up-selling, cross-selling, and co-promoting, you up the ante. You will increase your revenue, and make your customers stick like glue.

Sticking Points:

Here's the recap of the important points to remember about selling more to your current customers:

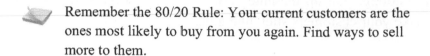 Remember the 80/20 Rule: Your current customers are the ones most likely to buy from you again. Find ways to sell more to them.

Follow the money: Find out what else your customers want to buy and find ways to provide it for them.

Up-sell! It's the easiest way to increase your revenue stream. If you're not up-selling, you're leaving easy money on the table.

Don't assume your customers know about everything you offer. Tell them regularly. Then tell them again.

Sharing success stories about how others have used your products allows you "sell without selling."

Don't balk if customers find unusual uses for your product. Figure out a way to capitalize on it instead and increase sales.

Explore every opportunity for joint ventures. It's a low cost/no cost way to expand your customer base.

Chapter Eleven:
Lost...and Found

Where'd They Go?

Repeat business speaks volumes about your company. After all, who would continue to use a company that didn't serve them well? Folks who buy based on price alone, who don't care about customer service, will only stick with you until they find what they want some place cheaper. They have limited LTV and probably aren't worth keeping. If you offer a fair price and killer customer service, you'll get and keep the sorts of customers who will grow your business.

Sadly, there will be times when you do, in fact, lose customers. This is a natural part of every business. Sometimes customers move, they go out of business (in a B2B situation), or some customers simply no longer have a need for your particular product or service. Certainly, these are some scenarios beyond your control as a business owner.

However, the losses you absolutely don't want to incur are those that you can and should control. One of the top reasons customers cite for leaving a business is **indifference**. It's my experience and belief that most customers will cease patronizing a business because of a bad experience with an employee, usually based on the employee's indifference. This is something you can control and want to avoid. How? Simple. Train your employees how to provide over-the-top customer service.

With *indifference* leading the list of top reasons that customers cite for leaving a business, it's easy to see why regular and frequent contact and over-the-top customer service are critical to your success and growth.

> **Sticky Note:**
> "If a company lost 10% of its inventory to theft, swift action would be taken to turn the tide. If a company is losing 10% of its customers to competitors, no one might even notice it." —Jon Anton, consultant for the center of Customers-Driven Quality, Purdue University, in West Lafayette, Indiana

However you lose a customer, remember that you don't lose the value of an average order; you lose that customer's lifetime value, which includes all future orders and any future new business from their referrals.

Lost-Customer Strategies

Sticking like glue to improve your profitability and grow your business is the goal. Let me be very clear: When you lose a customer, it is absolutely worth your time and effort to get them back. Why? By now, you know my answer is going to be "because of lifetime value, that's why," but that's only part of the story in this case. It's also important to know why customers left. If they've left because of a problem with your product or service, without knowing what it is, you can't fix it. If you don't fix it, there's going to be more holes in your bucket!

Learning why customers leave your business is the first step in plugging those holes. Once you know what's causing the holes, you can prevent them, and keep more water in your bucket, more customers in your business.

No doubt, it can be difficult to determine if a customer has left for good or is simply inactive for a period of time. There may be valid reasons for inactivity that are beyond your control, such as unemployment, illness, or a distracting personal situation.

A broad approach to this is to use what I refer to as a **"lost-customer campaign."** Such a campaign could and should include direct mail, e-mail, and perhaps phone calls.

You can send a "We miss you and want you back" **direct-mail** or **e-mail** message to customers who are inactive, and follow that up with a "Sorry we haven't heard from you" message. You may even choose to include an offer or a special discount to pique their interest and to incite them to purchase from you again.

Successful lost-customer campaigns are usually multi-step. Rarely is any marketing campaign successful with simply one effort to reach out.

The only real way to determine inactivity versus a truly lost customer is to make some **phone calls**. Sure, it can be time-consuming, and you may get an earful if customers were truly dissatisfied with your company. As unpleasant as such a phone call may be, you should relish these opportunities because the information you get will be incredibly valuable, and, in many cases, you will be able to solve whatever situation caused your customer to have these bad feelings in the first place.

Please keep in mind that what the customer tells you is not about right or wrong—this is about your customers' perceptions of how they were treated. Whether or not they were actually mistreated is not the point. If they believe they were mistreated, and choose not to spend one more dime with your business, who loses?

Listen to their complaints and be ready to rectify the problems. (Learn how below, in Apologies and Accountability!) It's best to script the calls, to a degree, for whoever makes the calls, and the person should be trained not to take anything personally. The call is about getting back, and keeping, more customers for life, for the good of the business.

You should be ready to offer lost customers an incentive to return. In addition, if you're hearing recurring themes from making lost-customer phone calls, you know you've got a problem that needs to be addressed, and addressed quickly.

Remember two things about these sorts of phone calls:

1) Politeness rules (it never pays to get into an argument and add fuel to an already burning fire).

2) Be prepared to act on the information you receive, or else you're simply wasting everyone's time, including your own.

It's important to know whether a customer is lost or is simply inactive for a period of time. Whether you use a high-tech solution like a customer relationship management software program, or telephone calls, or e-mails, or simply rely on your intimate knowledge of your customers and their buying habits, knowing when a customer truly leaves is powerful information and should be acted upon.

If you have a business where it is obvious when a customer leaves (and is not inactive), such as a membership program, *survey* past clients regarding their decisions to leave. Look for similar reasons, and fix them fast!

Sticky Note:
"The customers you lose hold the information you need to succeed." —Frederick F. Reichheld, director of Bain & Company, in Boston

Once again, I'll share a story that reflects this. With my No Hassle Newsletter program, it's critical for me to have a reliable printer and mail house. After all, I'm basing my reputation on the printer's quality and responsiveness. About a year ago, I switched

printers for my monthly mailing. I realize that I was probably not this national chain's largest customer; however, my order was not only sizeable, it was ongoing and repeated every month. What's more, by the very nature of what I was offering my clients, there was certainly a lot of room for growth for this vendor as I grew my business. Every new client I got with my program meant more business for the printer as well.

Simply by understanding exactly what I was offering to my clients, this printer should have quickly calculated that my lifetime value was probably larger than most of their clients, with a lot of potential for future growth. My reason for leaving really stemmed from indifference. I never heard one peep from the sales representative who courted my business in the first place. Not a "Hello, Jim, just wanted to touch base to see how things are going for you" or a "Are you satisfied with the service and quality you're receiving? I know you re-sell our product." Not a peep.

The failure to stay in contact with me screamed indifference, and that's not the kind of company I want to do business with.

Fast forward six months. I've switched to a new vendor. This time, I decided to use a local, independent printer. Now I really was a big fish for this vendor, and he was thrilled to win my business. It would be a large order month in and month out. After a couple months of production with a few minor glitches, which I brought to their attention, I realized that this printer was not properly positioned to offer the kind of quality and service I needed, so it was time to switch, and I'm happy to say I've found an outstanding vendor and I'm a raving fan. But guess what? I never heard one word from either of my former vendors after I left...after I joined the ranks of their lost customers.

If they'd bothered to check with me, they would have learned some valuable information about their business. Although I was not going to go back to either printer, they could have used what they learned from me to avoid losing future

customers. I represented a hole in both of their buckets that they probably could work to fix and avoid future lost customers.

I'm certain my reasons for leaving were not unique. It's probably a safe assumption that both of these printers spend some time each day complaining about their lack of business.

> **Sticky Note:**
> "There is only one boss. The customer. And he can fire everybody in the company from the chairman on down, simply by spending his money somewhere else."
> —Sam Walton

Checking the Math

When you lose a customer, you know you lose the lifetime value, as we've covered throughout *Stick Like Glue*, but wait…it gets worse. According to a *U.S. News and World Report* study regarding why customers leave, here are the statistics:

- 1% leaves because someone in the company dies
- 3% change location
- 5% make other friendships
- 9% go to the competition
- 14% are dissatisfied
- 68% leave because of bad service!

Wow—68% is a huge number, and the worst part is that a company's service is a completely controllable factor. Now you are really understanding the importance of the stick-like-glue message.

But hold on again, it gets even worse. In the same study, it was discovered that of the 68% who leave because of bad service (in this case, that percentage represents twenty-five people), the following happens:

- 1 customer complains.
- 24 are dissatisfied, but don't complain.

- 6 of the 24 non-complainers (one-fourth!) have serious problems.
- All 24 non-complainers tell 10 to 20 people about their bad experience.

So, if you've got 24 people who leave your company because of bad service, you stand the chance to have almost 250 to 500 bad reviews! And in this day and age when information truly travels at warp speed, you're setting yourself up for some real problems and headaches.

I told you that a testimonial can carry far more weight with prospects than your best marketing efforts. Well, the exact same thing is true of bad-mouthers. The people they complain to (your potential customers) are going to put more credibility in their first-hand bad experience than in all of your marketing messages.

Have you ever complained to friends, neighbors, and colleagues about bad service? I'm willing to bet that you have. I know I have. We all do. In fact, I know one woman who had a bad experience with an airline that lost her luggage. While she knows that's a regular problem, the error was exacerbated by the fact that she spent a week on a cruise without her suitcase. What made the problem even worse was the way in which the airline handled the problem—a lot of "It's company policy" rhetoric. While the initial problem was bad enough, they way they handled it (or failed to handle it) made it that much worse. It happened almost five years ago, and to this day, she won't hesitate to relate the story every time this airline's name comes up.

The message is simple: You absolutely cannot afford to offer bad service to your customers. They'll leave without complaining to you, but they will complain to a lot of other people. You end up losing sales and lifetime values, and ultimately you waste a lot of marketing dollars in feeble attempts to counteract bad word-of-mouth advertising. The worst-case scenario end result is a failed business.

Because this has the potential for such catastrophic consequences, it's critical to clearly explain to your staff what the numbers are, and what unhappy customers really mean to the overall health your business. I never hesitate to discuss real numbers (and I do mean real numbers, not theory) with my employees. It helps them make the clear connection between over-the-top service to create raving fans and the bottom line. They know a healthy bottom line is as important to them as it is to me.

Apologies and Accountability

In the study cited above about why customers leave a business, remember that there is *one* customer who will complain. As I mentioned before, the fact that customers take the time to complain signals that they want to continue their relationship with you, or else they'd simply be like the ones who walk away without saying a word. Well, that is, those who simply walk away don't say a word to *you*, but they don't hesitate to share a lot of bad words with a lot of other people.

Never ignore complaints. Meet them head-on. Here's a thought that will blow your mind: Look forward to and search out complaints! The reason is that too many customers don't complain because they don't like confrontation. They simply disappear, not to do business with you again. This is not good. No one enjoys listening to a complaint, but they signal that your customer took the time to discuss a problem rather than simply walk away. It's an indicator that they'd like to continue doing business with you…depending on the resolution.

In fact, a good complaint resolution can create very powerful word-of-mouth advertising. Conversely, a poorly handled complaint, or worse, an ignored one, goes a long way to fire up a customer beyond whatever the original problem was. Angry customers will tell about ten to twenty people about their bad experience, and they'll go out of their way to do so. On the other hand, only about two to three people will relate positive experiences, unless they're really over-the-top.

If you don't believe that, simply look at your own behavior. When was the last time you were angry at a company's product or service? Did you keep your frustration to yourself? I'd bet my bottom dollar you didn't. Now, when was the last time you were met with positive service? Did you tell anyone? Unless it was the over-the-top, out-of-the-box, put-a-huge-smile-on-your-face kind of customer service, you probably didn't mention it. If it was the kind of service I've been preaching about, I'm certain you told at least a few people about it!

The Internet makes it even easier for an upset customer to spread a bad report about you. If we had an upset customer in my early retail days, we would be worried about him or her telling twelve people (the average). Today, with the Internet, it's possible to for an upset customer to literally tell thousands and thousands of people within seconds. That's pretty scary, and a big reason my entire team and I work hard every day to address any concern or issue a customer or client may have.

Everyone on my support team knows three things:

1) They have the power to do whatever it takes to satisfy a customer without asking me. I have their backs.
2) They know I expect them to resolve a situation quickly.
3) They know that they can reach me anytime to jump in and talk with a customer if necessary.

While I'm proud that my Web sites have a large number of testimonials about how well my newsletters work, I am also proud of the testimonials that address the outstanding service we provide.

The way in which you handle the complaint can turn out to be more valuable in getting a customer to stick like glue than a lot of the other things you do in your business.

When you receive a complaint, immediately own up to the error and apologize. For some people, all they really want is an apology in the first place. If the problem is the fault of your vendor, it's still your problem, and you've got to take ownership of it. You're the one who selected the vendor to represent your company. Your vendor is an extension of your company. Period. When I had problems with my printer, I had to take the heat, and that's why I ended up switching. The quality and service reflected badly on me, and I couldn't control it.

Here's how I go about handling customer complaints:

1) First, I let them vent and blow off a little steam. If someone yells or curses at me, I let them know that I am going to fix the problem and make them happy, and politely ask that we have a calm conversation without yelling or cursing. Being empathetic is key to diffusing a difficult situation and a complaining customer. "Tom, I know you're angry about the damaged bike pump. I would be too." "I know you're frustrated because you son rode his new bike right into the curb and damaged the wheel. I would be too." *It's important to reiterate the problem to show that you understand it*, then your complaining customers won't feel like they are wasting time in addition to being angry about the problem in the first place.

2) Next, I let them know I have an idea for resolving the issue, but I ask what they think the fairest resolution would be. This really gives them a say in the situation, and also lets you know what they've got in mind. Remember, some people only want an apology; some want the apology *and* they want to avoid losing money. Almost always, my solution is going to be far beyond what they were going to ask for. In most cases, I'll offer and implement my solution anyway—it shows them I'm willing to really go over-the-top for them, and I'm on my way to creating a raving fan.

As I said, a well-handled complaint can do more than some of your best marketing. Many times, I end up getting unsolicited referrals like the ones I got from the billiard table incident. "Joe told me I would be crazy if I didn't shop here."

If you're worried that it will cost you too much money to allow complaining customers to suggest resolutions, forget about it. Since 98 percent of my customers (even the complaining ones) are honest, given the chance to state what they want, they almost always say something very reasonable.

This brings up another important sidebar strategy. Having a rock-solid **guarantee** is a must, especially if you have an Internet-based business. You're asking people to purchase without interacting with a human being, shaking hands, or looking into your eyes. It's a huge trust hurdle, and the best way to clear it is with a killer guarantee.

During my bike shop days, I developed an over-the-top strategy that drove my competitors crazy! No matter what brand of bike we sold, it came with our store's Lifetime Guarantee against any and all defects. While it was routine for most manufactures to offer a ten-year warranty on the frame and a one-year warranty on the parts, we gave our customers great comfort in telling them that we would back up every bike for *life*.

I'm guessing that you might be cringing right now, so let me explain my rationale. I figured that if a bike, or any part of it, was defective, it would certainly show up in the first few months, rather than years later. So, the chances that we would actually have to "eat" a warranty claim several years into the future were extremely remote. To me, this was a value-added strategy that customers loved, and we sold a lot of bikes with this level of extra protection.

My newsletter business guarantee is also very simple: If you're ever unhappy with the No Hassle Newsletter program, let me know immediately, and I'll refund your last monthly payment and stop the billing process. Simple and rock-solid. All the risk is on me.

With any Internet business, it's imperative to remove the perceived risk. That gains you customers by removing the distrust and worry of being scammed, and it sets you up to manage the expectation that you're out to make people happy. By offering a strong guarantee, I know I get many customers who were either sitting on the fence about their decisions or who wouldn't buy because of their uncertainty.

As for the extreme minority of people who may take advantage of you, my advice is to simply have a thick skin and roll with it. Oh sure, you can vent about it a little after you hang up the phone or after the customer walks out the door, but then let it go. You can laugh about the fact that your approach is working to grow your business, and despite these few difficult customers, you'll have more water in your bucket, more customers sticking like glue.

Sticky Note:

"What's the danger of giving away too much? Are you worried about having an over-satisfied customer? That's not much of a worry. You can forget about an over-satisfied customer, but an unsatisfied customer is one of the most expensive problems you can have." —Jan Carlxon, former CEO of Scandinavian Airlines Systems (SAS), Stockholm, Sweden

You've probably read the old business rules—Rule # 1: The customer is always right. Rule #2: When the customer is wrong, see Rule #1.

There's a lot of truth to that. Are you willing to go back to Rule #1 when your customers are the ones who are wrong? Obviously, I am. Think about how I handled the guy whose son damaged the bike wheel or the guy who'd run over his tire pump and told me it was defective. In both cases, there was no doubt in my mind that the customer didn't quite have their facts straight. But now you know my thinking: I've got two choices. Either I can be right, or I can take care of my customer and have a bigger bank deposit at the end of the day. Being right is not my highest priority. I'll choose the bigger bank deposit every time.

I won't say that I don't get a little irritated at times when customers aren't as "right" as they claim to be. However, my only focus is to keep my business growing and profitable for the long-term, and that requires me to have as many repeat customers, raving fans, and referrals as I can. And to the best possible degree, I work hard to limit those who are unhappy, whether it's through my fault or something they've done.

"You're Fired"

There are going to be a few customers that you simply cannot make happy, no matter what you offer or how hard you try. Some folks are just wired that way, so you may end up in a situation where it's best to "fire" your customer.

However, it's a very delicate situation and a real balancing act. You can't afford to have them go away angry, or you can end up with someone deriding your business on every blog and in every chat room they can find. Whether it's right or wrong, deserved or not, you cannot control this kind of customer, so you need to work hard to avoid it in the first place.

I've had situations in which customers complained, no matter what we did. If everything was letter-perfect, they'd go out of their way to nitpick, to find even the slightest thing with which to take issue. If the product was without fault, they'd complain about the invoice, and so on. You might have a few customers like that as well. If you handle it correctly, you can generate what I call a take-away sale.

I'd say that out of ten people who complain without what I consider to be a valid reason, in the end, I can get five to behave and become better customers by doing a take-away.

I'll typically say, "You know what? Given everything we've been discussing, I just don't think I have the level of service you're expecting or deserve, so I think it would be better if you found another vendor that can more effectively meet your needs."

It's amazing, but many will, after hearing that, start to retreat their position and backpedal in an attempt to save the situation—they're trying to not be fired! Given the prospect of having to search for a new vendor, they suddenly realize that they didn't have it so bad after all! Most of the customers who do retreat typically become very good customers.

For example, in my early days in business, I had a customer who bought my newsletter templates. After the $300 sale, he contacted me a few times with questions about making some alterations and changes. Although the package didn't include custom design changes, me being me and valuing over-the-top happy customers, I answered his questions and provided a few edits at no charge. After about the tenth question and request, I realized that there was likely nothing I could do to satisfy this customer, because he was expecting custom newsletter design service for a ready-to-go price. When I came to this realization, I decided to "fire" him. When I called him, I first apologized for all the trouble he was having with the newsletters. I knew it wasn't my fault and that he'd purchased something that was above his skill level. Regardless, I apologized. Remember Rule #2 when the customer is wrong.

Then I said, "In hindsight, this does not seem to be the right program for you. I'd like to refund all your money and let you select a program that will fit your needs better." I also suggested that he might want to try a more comprehensive program or even look for another vendor. His reply came very quickly, "Oh, no, no, this is fine, Jim. I can make this work; everything is okay."

By the way, I *always* offer a refund, no matter how hot-headed or obstinate a complaining customer may be. It's the only way I can even attempt to control what the person may go on to say about me.

While, on occasion, I might have the need to fire a customer, I do everything possible to ensure that no bad-mouthing occurs. If he or she is going to leave, I will do everything possible to make sure they have no bone to pick with me.

Getting back lost customers, or at the very least, finding out why they left, is worth the effort if you want to grow your business and be more profitable.

So if they're lost, find 'em, or find out why they left!

Sticking Points:

Here's the recap of the important points to remember about lost-customer strategies:

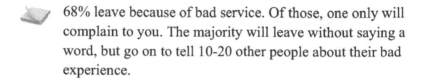

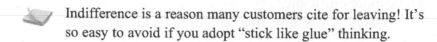

Indifference is a reason many customers cite for leaving! It's so easy to avoid if you adopt "stick like glue" thinking.

68% leave because of bad service. Of those, one only will complain to you. The majority will leave without saying a word, but go on to tell 10-20 other people about their bad experience.

With the power of the Internet and the ability for bad word-of-mouth advertising to go viral, you must do everything in your power to avoid it in the first place.

No matter who's at fault, apologize and take accountability for the problem. Most customers are only interested in getting an apology in the first place.

When you know customers are lost, find out why they left.

Don't waste your time determining that you lost customers if you're not going to spend time fixing the problem that drove them away.

Look for common problems, and fix them fast!

Sometimes you may have to "fire" a customer. If you handle it correctly, you can end up with a better-behaving customer and a take-away sale.

Your Glue

So there you have it—all the reasons why sticking like glue is the surefire way to grow your business, explode your profits, and tips on how to make your glue stickier. I sincerely hope that the ideas, strategies, and stories I've shared with you will encourage you to adopt the attitude of providing over-the-top, out-of-the-ballpark, put-a-huge-smile-on-their-faces customer service every time, to create raving fans of your business.

If you haven't thought about sticking like glue to your customers, now is the time to start. If you've been using a mediocre glue that doesn't adhere very well, I encourage you to do whatever it takes to make your glue stronger.

Make your glue as strong as the glue they used in that old commercial where the man's hard hat was glued to the steel beam. You'll be creating happy, trusting customers and raving fans, and will be generating repeat business and lots of referrals. It takes some work, but at the end of the day, you'll be on your way to significantly growing your business and your bank account.

Now it's up to you. Let me suggest the following action plan:

- I encourage you to focus on customer retention, not just customer acquisition. Fix the holes in your leaky bucket.
- Study your customer list to be certain you know where the gold is.
- Calculate your customers' average lifetime values and post that number prominently, so that you remember that a lost sale doesn't mean only that one occurrence.
- Get rid of any Ivory-Tower policies that you may have created, remembering that 98 percent of your customers are honest.
- Be easy to do business with, and strip away any barriers that you might have in place that prevent customers from giving you their money.

- Become the expert for them; figure out how to sell more to your existing customers.
- Go the extra mile to really stand out from your competitors.
- Create an effective loyalty/rewards program *and* make certain it's easy for your customers to cash in, because you'll be the ultimate winner.
- Create an effective referral program.
- Start gathering and using effective customer testimonials.
- Stay in regular, consistent, and meaningful contact with your customers, offering them something of value each time you contact with them.
- Be certain to ask "Would you like fries with that?"
- Follow the money. Go where the money leads.
- And finally, if you've got lost customers, find them, or find out why they left, and *fix* the problem.

With really good glue, I guarantee that running your business will be more enjoyable and more profitable. Please share your success *Stick Like Glue* success stories with me and I wish you the best of luck in becoming as sticky as you can possibly be.

Sticky Note:
"Your attitude, not your aptitude, will determine your altitude." —Zig Ziglar

Something Else about Jim

Jim's first book: *The Magic of Newsletter Marketing—The Secret to More Profits and Customers for Life*

Jim's wildly popular special report: *Use Newsletters and Grow Rich*, aka *Don't Be a Newsletter Pansy!* Get your free copy of this report at www.NewsletterPansyReport.com.

Check out Jim's following companies and products:

No Hassle Newsletters – www.NoHassleNewsletters.com
Newsletter Postcards – www.NewsletterPostcards.com
Jim's Entrepreneurial Success Kit – www.JimsSuccessKit.com
Newsletter Guru TV – www.NewsletterGuru.TV
Jim's Concierge Print and Mail on Demand Program – www.NewsletterPrintService.com

The Newsletter Guru's StandOUT E-zines
www.TheNewsletterGuru.com/ezines

Interested in hiring or learning more about Jim? Visit www.TheNewsletterGuru.com

About the Author

Jim Palmer is an entrepreneur, author, speaker, and coach to other entrepreneurs. Jim is the founder and president of Custom Newsletters, Inc. and is known internationally as The Newsletter Guru. For many entrepreneurs and business owners, he is the go-to resource for smart, effective strategies for maximizing customer relationships.

His companies and solutions include No Hassle Newsletters, Newsletter Postcards, The Newsletter Guru's Concierge Print and Mail on Demand Service, The Newsletter Guru's Entrepreneurial Success Kit, and Super Affiliate Pages.

Jim has been writing and designing newsletters for nearly thirty years for clients in just about every industry.

Several years ago, one of his clients was so over-the-top happy with his newsletter and the results that he telephoned Jim and said, "Jim, you are truly a newsletter guru!" Jim took it as a great compliment and has been using it in his marketing ever since.

Jim is a cancer survivor, has been married for thirty years, and has four grown children. He lives in Chester County, Pennsylvania with his wife, Stephanie, and their cat, Linus. Jim and Stephanie love to kayak, travel, and spend time with their family.

For more resources and information on Jim, his blog, and his companies, visit www.TheNewsletterGuru.com.

Bonus Chapter

Advanced Resources

As an added bonus for purchasing this book, I'm including the transcripts of two of my most popular entrepreneurial success videos, called "Massive Action" and "The Power of Zero." The strategies I describe in these two videos have been instrumental in the rapid growth of my business. While I invite you to watch these videos at my Newsletter Guru TV Web site, you can, if you prefer, read the transcripts that follow!

I'm also including the transcript from one of my monthly interviews. This interview was with Angela Megasko, the CEO of Market ViewPoint, a leading mystery-shopping company.

Again, if you'd like to see the original videos of Massive Action and The Power of Zero, feel free to visit www.NewsletterGuru.TV.

SUCCESS VIDEO ONE: MASSIVE ACTION
—by Jim Palmer

(RECORDED IN MY KAYAK!)

Well, hello everybody. This episode is coming to you from an early morning hour on the southern coast of Delaware. I'm going to pan real quick and just show you what I'm seeing here. These are some beautiful homes. We're staying as guests of some friends of ours down here. There's a boat going out, and the ocean is really, I guess, about a quarter mile on the other side of those trees. I found this little inlet right here, and I'm getting to go down there and get some early morning exercise, and I saw this sign saying "Slow No Wake." And let me tell you, when I saw slow, I don't like going slow. Slow bothers me. Even in a kayak I like to go fast. I prefer power. But you know what? In your business, slow is not always good.

I know in school we learned to plan. We learned slow. We learned deliberate, methodical steps is the best way, and that is not always the best way. Sometimes what's called for is massive action. And massive action is the ability to implement on many fronts, on multiple projects, simultaneously, not sequentially.

Now, the key strategy is, and this is kind of a mindset hurdle that you need to get over (anybody that's done massive action—it's a little bit scary and it's also a little bit messy); Dan Kennedy has an expression that says, "Success always leaves a messy kitchen." That's because you're doing fast things, multiple events, launching multiple projects simultaneously, not in any very neat order, okay?

So, if you're thinking of writing a book next year, maybe you're thinking of getting out an e-book, and next month you're going to write a special report, and maybe you're going to finally launch your blog. And then what else are you going to do? Oh, you're going to talk about doing a JV next quarter.

You know what? Scratch all of the calendars on those and get them done.

Hey, here's an idea. How about getting your book done in thirty days? How about launching that special report tomorrow, or the next day? How about reaching out to a few people before you close up shop today and get that JV going?

You know what? People that implement massive action, multiple projects simultaneously, those are the people that are achieving higher levels of success and higher levels of growth. And, yes, it does leave a messy kitchen!

I want to share with you, before we close out here, and I've got to blast down this beautiful waterway here, one of the things you need to get used to is that *good is good enough*. Again, I go back to my days in school when it's like there's a certain style of writing and everything has to be polished, and heaven forbid there's a spelling or grammar.

Now, you want your projects, you want your writings, you want your books to be as good as possible, yes. But if you keep striving for absolute perfection, zero mistakes, nothing gets done. The book will never get launched.

I heard Bill Glazer speak once, and he said, "Listen, if your book's on the bookshelf, and it's got a couple spelling mistakes, and it's a good cover, and people are compelled to buy it, you've sold a book. If the book is still in your word processor and you're looking and scrounging for every last error, nobody's going to buy it."

The idea, folks, is to make money, so get a thick skin. Somebody might shoot you an e-mail. Somebody may call you and talk about oh, I found an error. Well, correct it for the next thing. Correct for the next printing of books.

Get it done. Clean up your mess later. Plow forward. Don't be afraid to leave no wake. In fact, I want you to leave a wake. Get cranking. Crank up the speed. Change every deadline you have, and push it up and start implementing on multiple projects simultaneously. And I guarantee this time next year you're going to have higher levels of success.

This is Jim Palmer, The Newsletter Guru. I can't wait to see you next episode. I'm going to go get some early morning exercise, and I am going to leave a wake even in my kayak. Take care, everybody.

SUCCESS VIDEO TWO: THE POWER OF ZERO
—by Jim Palmer

(RECORDED IN MY OFFICE)

Well, hey everyone. In today's episode, I'm going to teach you about the power of zero. I first learned of this strategy, or it's actually a mindset shift, very early on when I started my business in late 2001.

Now, if you're familiar with my backstory, I had been unemployed for about a year previous to that. In the summer of 2001, I was first diagnosed with cancer. And so, in October of '01, when I decided to kind of get control of my life and start my business, I guess it's fair to say that my confidence and my goals were not huge. I was just happy to finally start my business and get going.

Now, I was very blessed to meet a gentleman, an older gentleman, a very successful entrepreneur who had started and grown at least three companies that I'm aware of. And he kind of took me under his wing, and he was I guess you would call my first mentor and coach. So we were meeting one day, and he said, "So, Palmer, what's your dream? What's your vision?"

I said, "Well," I said, "it's very simple. I'm just so happy to kind of start my business and get going." I said, "You know what, John? If I could generate $50,000 in revenue, I would be happy."

And he kind of looked at me with this look. It was kind of a combination of surprise, shock, and, actually, anger in his eyes. He said, "What the hell? $50,000? Dude, $100,000, $150,000...what's wrong with half a million?" He said, "Jim, could you live on half a million dollars a year?"

And I said, "Yes, I could."

He said, "Well, good. You need to think bigger." And he challenged me to kind of tear down the walls and kick down the door.

You see, here's what happens. I pretty much knew in order to generate $50,000 I knew how many networking events I'd need to go to, how many people I would need to meet, how many letters I might have to mail. In other words, it was pretty attainable. I knew the steps to do that. But to make, 100, 150, or a half a million dollars, that was completely different.

I then had to ask myself (once I grasped the logic and the theory of it; I wanted a much bigger thing) I needed to ask myself different questions starting with. "Okay, what do I need to do to make a half a million dollars?" And suddenly over the days, weeks, and months, it became very clear just mailing a few letters, shaking hands, going to networking events, chambers of commerce, things like that, that wasn't going to do it. I had to think on a much larger scale.

And, actually, one of the things that propelled me forward was meeting a few people that, actually, just came into my life, and I started developing this concept of, instead of selling just one newsletter to one customer, I would create these newsletter templates and sell them to hundreds of people around the country. And that soon became my second product, which was No Hassle Newsletters.

So that all started with me kicking down the door and opening up this bigger vision.

I'll tell you one more quick story. About a year ago after I had launched Success Advantage, which is my content and newsletter template program, another gentleman that I just highly respect and admire said, "where are you now?" I think at the time I was at about 40 to 50 subscribers. He said, "Where do you want to be?"

I said, "I want to quickly get to 100."

He said, "A hundred? What's wrong with a thousand?"

And, once again, my mind was challenged to think differently: *How am I going to get to a thousand?*

That's when I launched Success Advantage 2.0 where I added multiple newsletter templates. I added color, and black and white. I gave more content. I gave an e-zine template. I started adding more and more value and benefits to the program, and I've blasted past 100 subscribers.

And, because of that question go from 100 to 1000, that was when I nicknamed it "The Power of Zero. It's the power of thinking big.

So I want to challenge you, whatever your goal is, whatever you want to do, if you want to get five new clients this week, forget that. Go for 50.

It works, by the way, in savings also. Let's say you want to save 2 or 3 percent on your expenses. Don't do that. Save 30 percent. And guess what? If you fall short and only meet your goal by 50 percent and you save 15 percent, you're much farther along than if you made 100 percent of your original goal, which was just to save 3 percent.

Conversely, let's say you want to add 10 new clients this month. Forget that; go for 100. If you fall short and only get 50 percent and you add 50, you're much farther along than if you hit 100 percent of your goal to add 10.

So whatever your goal is, I want you to add a zero to it, and then start asking yourself the questions. Kick down the walls, throw down the door, and start asking yourself *What do I have to do to meet this new and bigger goal?* And you'll be surprised. Your mind will start feeding you the answers. You're going to start meeting people, and you're just going to be becoming aware of the different ways in which you can grow at a much more rapid rate, and to much higher levels of success.

So this is Jim Palmer, The Newsletter Guru, challenging you. Add a zero! I'll see you on the next episode.

By the way, I'm loving your comments and suggestions. I read every single one of them. Keep them coming, and we'll keep doing more episodes like this.

Take care, everybody.

The Newsletter Guru's
SUCCESS ADVANTAGE 2.0
MONTHLY COACHING CALL

AUDIO RECORDING TRANSCRIPT

Guest: Angela Megasko

Topic: The Importance of Mystery Shopping to Your
Business

Jim Palmer:
Well, hello there, everyone. This is Jim Palmer, the Newsletter Guru. I'd
like to welcome you to this call, the Success Advantage Coaching Gold
Call. I've planned a very special call this month, and we have an
extraordinary guest, Angela Megasko. She is the CEO of Market

Viewpoint, and I'll be properly introducing her soon. Angela, are you on the line?

Angela Megasko:
I am, Jim.

Jim Palmer:
So, we're ready to get with tonight's topic. And I think that even while times are tough, and if you watch the news, it's even worse than it really is. I think that there are many opportunities for entrepreneurs and business owners to not only survive, but actually thrive, in this economy.

Now, let's talk about some of the things that you can do to make sure that, first of all, you're on top of your game, and for the most part, I'm talking about your mental game. You know, for one thing, I strongly encourage you to turn off the news. Lee Milteer is an author that I respect and admire, and she has a great newsletter, and she's recently been talking about mindset issues. And in her recent one, there was a whole article about avoiding negativity. You know, kind of "we are what we eat," so to speak, and when you feed a lot of negative information and negative news, which is all about what the news channels are like, the radio, the papers, because that's how they sell subscriptions and get an audience. Good news doesn't sell. And you're just exposing yourself to so much negativity. It affects the way you think about your pricing, your customers, and it just really affects if you're going to roll out a new product, and things like that.

I want to tell you that I have been practicing what I'm now preaching for two weeks now. In fact, the day after the election is when Stephanie and I flew out to the St. Louis info summit. And since that day, I have not watched TV news of any kind. I've not read a paper. I told you I cancelled those about a month ago. And I don't even listen to talk radio anymore.

I'm either listening to Glazer-Kennedy CDs, or some other CDs, or music, or I'm listening to nothing. And I have to tell you that after two weeks, I don't know if you've ever tried to kick coffee or anything like that, I feel completely different. I feel positive. It's just really, really been a pleasure. It's not always easy. I kind of sometimes feel like I should get the remote in my hand and see what's going on, but trust me, you'll get enough about what's going on just because of the world, and the environment, and once in a while you pass a TV at the gym or something like that. So I encourage you to give that a try.

A few months ago, this is kind of getting on the recession and all, I remember reading about two months ago, three months ago, I saw a lot of entrepreneurs, including myself, say things like "I choose not to participate when you're talking about the bad economy." I think now that there's been so much happening over the last couple of months that if you say something like that, I think you kind of sound uninformed. And smart marketers are embracing kind of the general fear that is out there, and they're providing solutions for their customers and clients.

One of the things to recognize is that your customers, if they're watching the news, they're actually frightened. They're worried about losing clients, and growing, and their profits. They're actually looking for a savior, because most people in this situation, they don't know what to do. And, again, they get real worried. I think the majority of frightened people kind of look for outside help instead of looking at their own devices. And this is where, I think, there is a huge opportunity for you as a smart marketer, or whatever your business or your product offers. If you can be a hero to your customers ,and provide solutions that help them not to lose clients and customers, and actually gain new customers, you're going to be a lot better off than a lot of folks who are kind of pulling back and stopping their marketing and things like that.

Dan Kennedy, you probably know Dan, he's a very much a marketing guru to me. He has a formula, as you know, called problem-agitate-solution. That's where you kind of identify your problem, you agitate it, and then you prove a solution. And what he says in this economy is that you need to state the crisis in the worst, most graphic and dramatic way as possible, and agitate the fear so you get people really worried. You actually invalidate all of the solutions except yours. In other words, when you're writing sales copy or certain ads, or even the way you're talking, you want to present yourself as the one with the absolute solution and the best way that's going to help them.

Then, the next part of the equation is presenting yourself as uniquely capable with the solution. So I want to encourage you to be in more contact with your customers than you've ever been in the past. If you've struggled with a monthly newsletter, this is certainly the time to get that in gear. A monthly newsletter is just a vital part of maintaining customer relationships. And during these times of struggle, it's just very important to reach out in other ways, such as the telephone, or if it's geographically feasible for you, then do personal visits to your customers.

It's important that you know exactly what your customers are thinking and feeling. And it's equally important that they know you are someone who cares about them.

Now, as business owners, there are some things that we can do, and I'm going to go down a list real quickly here in about six minutes, and then I'm going to bring Angela on the call. But here are a couple of things that you can do. They're actually good things to do all year long, but sometimes it takes a little crisis to jolt us to action.

Number one, look for ways to add more value in what you're doing. Now, I whole heartedly believe in this strategy all the time. And, as an example, a couple of months ago, I began looking for ways to add more value to my various products and solutions. That's actually when I started adding my first template with Success Advantage. And two months ago, I added an e-zine template, just something else to help my customers communicate better. And now I'm going to be providing a B2B template, as I mentioned. Then I'll be announcing a print and mail on demand service.

So the point of this is that every month, or every other month at the outside, I'm finding different ways to add more and more value. And that's really a good way to keep customers from leaving you.

Another thing you can do, and these are kind of going back to you as an owner/operator, is reduce the interruptions in your life, and just really stay focused on everything that you can do to nurture your customer relationships. Get to know them. Get to know what they're feeling and what their pains are.

Another thing is look for customers who are actually looking for you. If you can identify customers who may be hurting with whatever your product or service is, find new and creative ways to go out there and draw them in.

Another thing I want to mention is being authentic. This is a time to be who you are. I believe most people are good and they care about their customers. They've started a business because they want to help others. You've got to let that show through.

The other thing is to be respectful, and I think that means being respectful of people's time. So if you do go visit a customer, let's say if they're in retail, you don't want to obviously stand there waiting around while they're taking care of business. Call first, or if you do stop in, again, just be respectful of their time.

Another thing that I try and do, is I do one thing every single day to bring in new business. That may be following up on a lead. It may be generating some kind of quote. It may be putting out a new e-mail series. Whatever you're doing, do at least one thing, every day, to bring in new business.

Probably one of the most valuable things you can do is remove the risk from people doing business with you. That generally refers to offering a very strong guarantee. In other words, if you're going out there and trying to get new clients, which is always a good idea, make it super easy, a kind of a no-brainer. You will take care of all their questions, their comments, etcetera. And when you can do that, in other words, make it a no-brainer, take away all the risk, I think you'll find it's going to be a little bit easier to close a sale.

Now, another important strategy is what I call "taking a close look at how your company is currently functioning," how it is perceived to be functioning by your customers, which a lot of us don't know that, frankly. I can tell you that I spent over twenty years in retail, as you know, if you've read my back story. You know I started in the bike shop. And what you think is going on in your business is seldom the case. I mean your mission statement, your plans, your expectations, what you think is going on with the way your business is being run, all rest squarely on the shoulders of your frontline staff, and if you're a solopreneur, that actually includes your voice mail, your e-mail, your Web site, everything that is how they're interacting with you.

Now, to address this topic, I wanted to bring on the nation's leading authority on mystery shopping and business assessments. Angela Megasko is the president and CEO of Market Viewpoint, which is a professional mystery-shopping firm dedicated to the growth and profitability of the clients they serve.

Now, in business circles, I think this is really cool, Angela is known as Jane Bond, which is a nickname kind of acquired because, in the spy world, she's known as the Jane Bond of the secret shopping world. So I always preach about having a good character, so I think that's really cool.

Now, her client list is very long, and it includes even some top organizations, such as the Panasonic Corporation, Goddard Schools, which is a huge multi-unit school complex, Petco, which is a national retailer of pet food, Burlington Coat Factory, Longwood Gardens, Waterloo Gardens, just to name a few.

Angela works with over 100,000 mystery shoppers, which, I think, must be just an insane thing to juggle. I'm sure she's got systems for that. And the data that she collects through working with her mystery shoppers, she's able to provide advice and produce real, competitive advantages for her clients.

So, Angela, welcome to the call. I very much appreciate you making time for us.

Angela Megasko:
Thanks, Jim. It's a pleasure to be here.

Jim Palmer:
Excellent. As I like to do, I put myself in the customer's shoes, and I kind of came up with some questions that I think the folks listening on the call, and later on the CD, would like to hear.

So, here's question one. I know you're in touch with a lot of organizations out there. You have several clients, huge corporate clients and even some local clients. So, can you give us a flavor? Let's turn off the news, and give us a flavor of what's actually happening out there. How are business owners responding to this economy?

Angela Megasko:
Well, Jim, it's like anything else. People are responding in a variety of ways. And what we're finding is that people are actually falling into one of two categories, generally speaking. And the first category is what I'm going to call "the complainers." These are the people who are not doing well right now, and they're looking for any excuse to blame it on. So the economy is definitely the major excuse for these businesses that are not doing extremely well right now.

Then you have the other camp of people, that other category, and these are businesses that are being extremely creative at finding ways to add value to their existing product line, or their service line for their existing clients, and to attract new clients into their business. And I'm amazed at some of the things that some of the people are able to do out there. And when I talk about adding value, and, Jim, I know you do a really, really good job with all of the products that you provide to your clients—

Jim Palmer:
Thank you.

Angela Megasko:
—I'm often amazed at the things that people get when they're
purchasing products and services from you. But one of the things that I
think is extremely important for people listening on this Success
Advantage Gold Call is for them to understand that, in a down economy,
customers don't stop spending. They just spend smarter.

And by that I mean that they seek out value. And it's kind of like when
you need shampoo, and you go to the grocery store, and you're walking
down the health and beauty aids aisle, and you spot your brand. And you
go over to the brand of shampoo, and you find the packaging that you
usually buy, but right next to it, for the exact same price, there's another
bottle that has 25 percent more. What do you do? You grab the bottle
with the 25 percent more, because you perceive that it has greater value.

So, every dollar that our customers are spending in today's marketplace,
they're expecting that they're going to get $2 worth of products and
services out of that one dollar that they're spending. So they're trying to
be very smart.

Jim Palmer:
Yeah, you said some really powerful things. I want to make sure
everybody hears and understands what you just said there. One of the
things I think always kind of irritates me, because I tend to be a positive,
forward-thinking guy, is that a lot of people that you run into at
networking events and different places like that, there is always
something to blame. Oh, the economy sucks, or the competition is this,
that, the people who are working for me… I mean, there are people that
always have excuses, and I think, for a large part, those are people that
look at the glass half empty. I'd say the people on this call are smart,
because they're actually subscribing to something. They're listing to this
call because they want to learn and do better. So there's an opportunity
there.

Again, going back to my retail days when I used to do training, I used to
tell people, "Customer service is so bad, and I think it's gotten worse."
But I used to tell people, Customer service is so bad, that if you simply
are polite, you smile, and you address their basic needs, you've got a
homerun."

Angela Megasko:
It's true.

Jim Palmer:
Just to give you an idea, a couple of weeks ago, I was shopping for an accessory for my iPod, my iTouch. And I went in to kind of a name brand store, big box store that everybody would know, and I just could not get service. I did have a couple of questions I was not able to determine from the display, and I could not get anybody to wait on me.

When I to go walk and find somebody, instead of saying, "Sir, I'll be with you in a minute" or whatever, he said "I'm already working with two people." And I said, "Well, then two people is what you'll be left with," and I left the store and I went somewhere else.

I think that's another example that people will still spend, because I see people out in the shops. I see them in the mall. I see them in the office supply stores. People are still spending, but I think you're right, people are searching for smarter ways to purchase. But they're also looking for companies and businesses that simply say "I appreciate you, thank you for coming in. How can I help you?"

Angela Megasko:
They care, right?

Jim Palmer:
They care, and I just think that's huge. Now, let me ask you another question, Angela. How do you go about, from the initial time you get a client and then you're engaged in the whole mystery shopping strategy, how do you actually identify what your customers want? And I say that about you and your company, but how do you also identify what your clients' customers want so you can give them feedback?

Angela Megasko:
Well, being in the market research field, it's perfect for giving you that inside information, or that ability to be inside the mind of your customer in order to deliver the products and services that they want, because that's really why we're in business. You know, we're not in business to produce something that we want. We're in business to produce something that our customers want and will purchase.

Jim Palmer:
Right.

Angela Megasko:
So, when my customers come to me and say, We think we want to set up some sort of a mystery shopping program," or "We think we want to do some research," I'm thrilled, because I know they're spending their

money wisely. And I say the best way to identify what your customers want is to ask them. And in today's market, that becomes even more important, because as quickly as things are changing for us and our businesses, they're changing just as rapidly for your customers. And it's important for us to lockstep with our clients, so that we can partner with them as best we can to make sure that the market's staying satisfied.

Jim Palmer:
And how do you go about doing that? How do you identify what the customers are thinking, what they're seeing, how they're perceiving? And then how do you report that actually to your clients?

Angela Megasko:
Well, there are a couple of different ways that we do it. And, again, it depends on what our client's need is. Occasionally, we will embark on mystery shopping programs for customers or secret shopping. For your listeners who may have been in retail, or in the restaurant industry, at some point in their lives, they will be extremely familiar with the concept of mystery shopping or secret shopping, because it's been around for a really long time. It's been around since the 1940s.

Sometimes the problem that our customers have really requires more customer surveys or employee surveys or vendor surveys.

Then at times, we'll recommend focus groups because our client may be interested in launching a new product or a new service. And before they put an awful lot of money into R & D, they want to make sure that there's a viable market out there for their new idea.

Jim Palmer:
Wow, I had no idea you did that, Angela. That's really cool. So let me interrupt you real quick. A lot of the people on the call, now you have so much experience working with big companies, big chains. I know you do a lot of work with banks. But a lot of folks that are going to be hearing this CD, Angela, are kind of entrepreneurs, solopreneurs. Some may have a small staff. Folks like myself have virtual assistants, which are not employees, but they are people that work for me and, in some cases, have access to my clients and customers. Can you work, and does your company work with folks like myself and people on the call?

Angela Megasko:
Absolutely. We work with companies of all sizes, because we all have a need to be in touch with our customers. And sometimes when you think about it, people will say to me, "Well, I don't have a big budget, so how

can I get the information that I need from my clients, because at this point in time, I'm still relatively small." And what I'll say is, "Look, if you're on a tight budget, it's still important for you to ask your customers what they need, and what they want, and what they expect from you."

So engage in dialogue with your customers. I mean, it can be something as simple as an informal question and answer session that you have with your existing clients. And you can weave these informal Q and A sessions into the end of telephone calls. You may be on a telephone call with a client about an unrelated issue, and at the end of the call, you ask your client if they have a few seconds. But you just want to find out how you're doing as a company, and find out what kinds of products and services they may be requiring of you in the future, so that you can be prepared to help them in whatever way you can.

At the end of the meeting, if you're in a face-to-face meeting with a client, take them out for a cup of coffee afterwards and engage in some dialogue with your customer, again, to make sure that you're lockstep with what their needs are, and to make sure that you're meeting those needs.

So you don't necessarily have to be a big company to ask the questions that you need to ask in order to deliver the products and services that your customers want.

Jim Palmer:
Well, that's great. I know a few days ago, when I was talking to your assistant and getting us all scheduled, one of the things I asked her was about working with small companies. And she mentioned something that I didn't even realize, which is, for small companies like entrepreneurs, solopreneurs, you actually review like Web sites and voice mail and things like that. I'd like to hear a little bit about that. I was fascinated when I heard that.

Angela Megasko:
No problem. I'm glad you brought it up, because another important point for the Success Advantage Gold Call listeners tonight is to understand the importance of evaluating all the portals of entry that a customer or perspective customer would have and to get into your business system. And it's complex today. They can reach you through Web sites. They can reach you through e-mails. They can get to you through telephones or call centers. Or, if you happen to be in the kind of job where you've got a bricks and mortar location, they may even be stopping by physically to do business with you. And so, in those situations, you want

to make sure that every way a customer has access to you, you want to make sure you're evaluating all of those portals of entry.

Call yourself once in a while and listen to what your on-hold message sounds like. Go to your Web site from time to time and make sure that your information is up-to-date and it's accurate. It's important to make sure that no matter how big your company is, that you're checking all of these avenues of approach.

Jim Palmer:
When your assistant told me about checking and screening voice mail, kind of the answer you just gave, I actually hung up and listened to my own message. I recorded it well over a year ago, and I recognized that I was promoting an old Web site. And I thought, holy smoke! So that's some really good advice and suggestions there.

How often do you suggest doing kind of a mystery shopping? It probably depends on the size of the company, but do you have kind of a rule of thumb as to how often someone should use a company like yours?

Angela Megasko:
It really depends on your business. And when customers ask me that, or when prospective customers ask me that, I'm always very clear that a lot of it depends on things like your staff turnover. You know, places like McDonald's, for example, they have a pretty high staff turnover. They deal with a younger employee population that really is only there temporarily. I mean, those kids aren't there as a career, for the most part. They're there for summer jobs and part-time jobs.

So, if you have a workforce that turns over on a fairly regular basis, I recommend mystery shopping on a fairly regular basis. And by that I mean either weekly or monthly. But if you're in a fairly static environment where things don't change all that much or that quickly, then some mystery shopping programs will be either quarterly, sometimes we'll evaluate twice a year, three times a year. It usually depends on budget, most certainly, and the kind of business that you're in. So that's a general rule of thumb.

Jim Palmer:
Yeah, I think once a year is probably the minimum. You know the business, but I think a couple times a year. Things happen so fast. Things change. Again, for me, Web sites change, different things. It's probably something to do. It's kind of like changing a battery in your smoke detector with the seasons or the time change. It's kind of something like

that. I'm really fascinated. You said you do focus groups for product launches and things like that, but I've also heard that focus groups can be kind of expensive. So, is that true, even though there's probably high value there, or can you address that for me?

Angela Megasko:
They can be, but they don't have to be. There's a lot of ways to make sure that the cost, the price tag on a focus group, doesn't go through the roof. But I think when you take a look at the price of gathering the data, and doing the research pre-launch, and the potential for developing something that your market isn't interested in and having a failure of a product, I think the research itself it just pays for itself, because you're able to identify those things that the market is interested in.

There are a couple of rules of thumb that I like to tell people about focus groups. And some companies opt to do their own focus groups, which is fine. But I say use a third party to facilitate this, so that you as the owner of the company can observe. There are some companies out there that have the one-way mirrors and, as the owner of the company, you're on one side of the mirror and you can observe what's happening while the focus group is being conducted. If you use a third party, it allows you, as the owner of the company, to be able to sit back and watch people's body language, and to be able to listen to the responses, and not get caught up in the detail, and the operational components of actually conducting the focus group and facilitating it.

If you make a list of the questions that you want to ask, it's important for you to let go of what you think the answers should be, and for you to let go of what you think the outcome of the focus groups can be. Because a lot of times, and we've seen it happen, you go in thinking one thing, and what your market tells you is something completely different. For example, you may think that the product that you need to develop should be the color red, but by the end of the focus group you find out that it really should be purple, because that's what the market is looking for.

So you really need to go in with an open mind and an open heart, and really listen to what the customers are requiring of you, and what it is that they're hoping you'll provide.

Jim Palmer:
Boy, that's huge. That really makes me think a lot. A couple of things you said there, with the owner being on the other side of the glass, I think, in addition to watching the body language, even though people know they're probably being watched, having the owner in the room, I

think will kind of color some of the comments. I'm just kind of guessing here. You're the expert. But I'm thinking that you might not get really true and accurate, honest feedback if you're actually in the room with the focus group.

Angela Megasko:
Bias could be built in, especially if you're a well-known company with a well-known product or a well-know service. So, to have that division between yourself, or your management team, or people from your company, to be divided by that mirror or by that wall, is important because you do want people to be honest, and you want them to be candid. So it is important to make sure that bias isn't a part of the process. And by having a third party conduct it, you're eliminating at least some of that bias.

Jim Palmer:
Yeah, and something else that you said kind of rings true with everything we hear and we're taught by Dan Kennedy and Bill Glazer is that so many people will actually set out to build their product. It's the ultimate product. Then they go out and try and sell it, when, in fact, the worst case is there might not even be a market for it.

Angela Megasko:
Exactly.

Jim Palmer:
Or it could be as easy as, like you said, it's a different color, different price point. It includes different things. And, therefore, it's going to be easier to sell. So I think this whole thing about focus groups and market research is very, very important. I know as entrepreneurs, myself included, we kind of suffer sometimes from the shiny object syndrome. We're off chasing this new idea, and we're getting it to launch, and getting the whole product launch going. The next thing you know, well, it turns out there wasn't much of a demand for it. So I think that's some really good advice.

Now, let me ask you how you communicate the information that you get from the focus group, because I'm sure a lot of times the owner or the president of the company is not there. So how do you then take all that and communicate what you learned to the customers?

Angela Megasko:
Well, it depends, and I'll say that whether you're gathering your research, your data, through the focus group component, whether you're

conducting occasional surveys of your existing client base, employee surveys, vendor surveys, or whether you're performing mystery shopping and you have a mystery shopping program in place, I think the thing that is important is that the data is coming back, if the studies are being conducted, the surveys are being conducted by a good, solid, market research firm that knows what they're doing, basically what's coming back is of value.

It allows you to determine what is it about your company that makes people want to do business with you. And for some companies, it could be the years of experience that they have, because for some customers and consumers that's important. You'll see some of those things on taglines, "Doing business since 1856" or whatever. For others, it's ease of use, that you're a very easy company to do business with. That's important for some people, and it seems to be more and more important as times goes on, because time is so important to all of us that we just want it to be easy.

Jim Palmer:
Absolutely. We have about five or six minutes before the Q and A, and I have two more questions that I want to try and get in.

Angela Megasko:
Sure.

Jim Palmer:
So let's say I know you, and I know you have kind of a survive-and-thrive mindset. So how did you develop and foster this within your organization? So how could other people learn to do that?

Angela Megasko:
I think we all, as entrepreneurs, I think we're a very special breed of people to begin with. And I think you almost have to have that survive-and-thrive mindset just to get through the day sometimes. But I think one of the things that I've always lived by, is that I do not practice or accept mediocrity. There is too much of that in this world. And I think in order for, certainly, my firm to stand out, we have to be doing business better than the competition, and we have to be providing more value than the competition. So the fact that we don't practice or accept mediocrity is just something that we live by, because there's just too much of it out there.

So I think the other thing that is important to me, Jim, is that I sort of have this crazy belief that opportunity is all around us. I believe that treasure is buried and hidden all around me, and I just have to find it. And I think even during these economic times, there is opportunity in this crisis that we're going into, and there is treasure here. It's up to all of us as entrepreneurs, because I really believe it's that entrepreneurial spirit that's going to save our economy. But all we have to do is find those treasures, find those opportunities, those pockets of opportunity, for us to be able to make it through these difficult times and come out on the other side so much richer for having gone through the experience. And I'm not necessarily talking financially richer, but certainly richer in terms of the experiences that we had and what we learned from them.

Jim Palmer:
Yeah, you know it's all what I like to call tuition, which is, it's your education.

Angela Megasko:
Oh, I like that.

Jim Palmer:
There are no such things as mistakes, just experiences and lessons. It sounds like you are actually, with your phraseology, quoting that famous book *Acres of Diamonds*. I don't know if you were or not, but that's an awesome book.

Angela Megasko:
A great, great book.

Jim Palmer:
Good. My last question, Angela, is I know you work with some Fortune 500 companies. What are some of the things that our folks on the call can learn from how you work with Fortune 500 companies?

Angela Megasko:
Well, because I'm in the information-gathering business, I like to ask people what they're doing and what some of their best practices are, which allows me to pass some of those best practices along to other companies, and to other individuals to help them.

So, some of the best practices that are happening out there right now are the fact that companies are giving out a lot of freebies; it's the buy one get one. People are looking for something for nothing. So we really need to be prepared to be giving a little bit more right now. And what we need to be prepared to give away is our best stuff, because people are going to remember that. When the market turns around again, people are going to remember that.

Jim Palmer:
If I can interrupt you without losing your train of thought, remember the other bullet you want to do. That's really critical, especially for information marketers, people who do business on the Web site. It's so important that you just give good information, whether it's through auto-responders, or free reports, or whatever. The more you can educate your prospects about who you are as a company, what you stand for, where your expertise is, and how you can help solve their pains, that's how you're going to get a customer. That's a great strategy that I know you're talking most brick and mortar and big companies, but that's a strategy that the folks on our call can use for sure, so sorry to interrupt you again.

Angela Megasko:
No problem, no problem. One of the other things that we're finding that people are doing is that they're doing a lot of customer pampering. There's a shopping mall located not terribly far from where I live. One of the things that the mall is doing is they're giving free chair massages to their shoppers on Saturdays and Sundays, because people are so stressed out right now and life is stressful. Then you couple that stress with a downturn in the economy, and suddenly people get real crabby and real stressed out real quick.

So, it's finding ways to tell your customers that they're special, and that you value them, by finding ways to make life easy for them. So this shopping mall feels that chair massages are a nice way to demonstrate that.

Jim Palmer:
That's awesome. You know, there's somebody that's fairly prominent in the Glazer-Kennedy world, Dr. Charlie Martin. He's in Richmond, Virginia. And he has a dental practice that probably you could equate it to the best country club. I believe he's got a grand piano in there. There's like a coffee bar. I mean, people are pampered beyond belief.

Angela Megasko:
That's great.

Jim Palmer:
He's also known for having one of the most expensive dental restoration practices. But you know what? People will pay to be pampered, and they

appreciate being pampered. And when it comes down to where you are going to spend your money, it's "Who is going to pamper me? I work hard for my money, and I want to be taken care of in a fashion that I want to be taken care of." So I really appreciate that comment. I appreciate all the great advice you've got, so thank you.

Let me just unmute the calls here. Okay, we are live. If anybody has a question to ask, you can do so. I do have like three questions to get to here. So just speak up if you're on the call.

Right now, though, I have a question from Rodney in Atlanta. He wants to ask Angela how your service can help someone with a home office and no staff. We sort of covered that earlier, but do you want to give that one a try Angela?

Angela Megasko:
Well, a lot of times when we're dealing either home-based businesses or companies that have a smaller operating environment, we talked a little bit before about actually having these spies or pretend customers, actually take a look at things like your Web site. Take a look at things like e-mailing you to find out how quickly you respond, and the tone of your e-mail responses, which is an incredible art. Think about this. One of the easiest ways for us to communicate with each other as human beings is face-to-face. We're not operating in an environment where, socially, there are not a lot of face-to-face encounters anymore. A lot of our business encounters are by telephone and by e-mail.

So, when we communicate by phone or e-mail, we're certainly losing the body language ability that we have as human beings to talk with each other and to understand each other. When we communicate by phone, we lose the body language. When we communicate with e-mail, we not only lose the body language, but we also lose the ability to hear how someone is saying something.

Jim Palmer:
Yeah, I've always preached, Angela, with e-mail, the less said the better, because you could say something in an e-mail an in your head you're kind of saying it one way. You even hear yourself with your voice inflection. Someone reading the exact same word in an e-mail goes, "What's wrong with him. Did I tick him off, or is he ticked off with me?" and things like that. So it's kind of dangerous.

Angela Megasko:
Exactly.

Jim Palmer:
Your answer is kind of wandering right into the next question, which is
from Beth, who is a new subscriber this month. So welcome, Beth.

Angela Megasko:
Hi, Beth.

Jim Palmer:
Yeah, she sent this question via the Web link. She's actually listening
online. She has four virtual assistants that interact with her clients. So
they're kind of the frontline. "How would you suggest checking up on
their interaction, which is mostly through e-mail?"

Angela Megasko:
Well, again, we could certainly plant a couple of mystery shoppers to
interact with those virtual assistants. But I think, probably, in Beth's
situation, actually surveying her customers is a great idea, to actually pull
together a short survey. It doesn't have to be long. It doesn't have to be
drawn out. It can be very short. It can be very simple. She can give her
customers a little something for taking the time to fill the survey out for
her. It could be a gift certificate. It could be coupons for something, as a
way of saying thank you to her customers for taking the time. But I
would think that a customer survey would probably be a really great way
for her to assess how her virtual assistants are doing.

Operating in the virtual arena, she's very, very wise to want to ask her
customers how these virtual assistants are doing, because they're not in
our corporate space. We can't hear how they're interacting. We can't see
how they're interacting. And while we can tell our assistants that we
want them to behave and conduct business in a certain way, they're
virtual. And so the control is gone, and the best way is to either mystery
shop or to survey your customers to find out how those assistants are
doing. So I think that's very wise to be concerned about that.

Jim Palmer:
Another thing, and I'm not sure what the whole setup is with their
computers, I mean, a lot of virtual assistants are not really connected to
the office or corporate headquarters, so to speak. But there is a way when
you are communicating with your computers together is to check up on
e-mails or ask that any correspondence that they send out is blind copied
to Beth or whoever the owner/operator would be.

I don't think there's anything wrong with, especially if they know up
front, some e-mails will be reviewed for training purposes when you're

calling the customer service center. I think the strategy that I use with my folks is that they blind copy me or, in some cases, will just cc me on all correspondence. So I get to see a lot. I skim it and I just kind of look for things.

Angela Megasko:
Good protocol.

Jim Palmer:
I might actually send back an e-mail to them and say, "Great answer, but here's how I might answer it next time," or something like that. So it's kind of a good training one.

This question, actually, came in earlier this week via e-mail from Derek. He's one of our Internet national subscribers. When I announced you were going to be on the call, he sent this e-mail. And he said, "I am an information marketer whose primary method of operation is the Internet, so I have very little actual interaction with my customers. How would you suggest I find out how my service is being perceived by my online shoppers?"

Angela Megasko:
I love the idea, again, of surveying those folks. Because your business is online, Derek, and your customers are used to operating in that environment with you, and communicating with you that way, I love the idea of your pulling together a survey and asking them to fill that out for you online. You'll gather lots of great data on how you're performing, how your clients perceive the product or service that you're offering, and what's the likelihood that they'll continue to do business with you going forward.

Another thing that I think is a really great question to ask them is if there are any needs that they currently have that are not being met.

Now, another suggestion that I might have for you is that if you have telephone numbers, or ways of communicating with these clients, possibly by telephone, or even by mail, that you think about the possibility of sort of expanding that research to include maybe a certain percentage of telephone surveys, because a lot of times with online surveys, clients don't have the opportunity to interact with you. You don't have the opportunity to interact with them. They may give you an answer about something, but then you don't have the opportunity to ask them what they mean by that.

So I like the idea of maybe doing a certain percentage of telephone surveys as well, which I think would be a really, really great idea, and very comprehensive.

Jim Palmer:
Yeah, wow. Gosh, we're almost out of time. I can't believe how fast these hours go by. I want to thank Angela for her time and her terrific advice tonight. Angela, thank you so much for being on the call.

Angela Megasko:
Jim, it was a pleasure.

Jim Palmer:
Oh, great. Now, listen, if someone wants more information about what you and your company Market Viewpoint offer, how can they get in touch with you?

Angela Megasko:
Oh, gosh, it's easy. We live in a communication age. Well, they can certainly see and read more about what we do by visiting us online, and that is www.MarketViewpoint.com. If folks want to e-mail me, I'm easily reached at angela@marketviewpoint.com. And I have a toll free number and they can reach me at 1-888-942-7030. That's 1-888-942-7030.

Jim Palmer:
Excellent. And do you have any kind of special report or any kind of information? If people do get in touch with you, do you have something going on for our callers tonight?

Angela Megasko:
We do. We do. As a matter of fact, we are offering, because we believe so, so strongly in the power of customer retention, always but especially in this market. I mean, some are saying they're concerned about whether or not they'll get any new clients in the next year, maybe even two years, based on what's being predicted.

So we believe so strongly in customer retention, and we want our clients to have strong customer retention plans in place, that we're offering a thirty- minute, complimentary telephone consultation to review your customer retention strategy in your business. We'd be delighted, delighted to work with you on that.

Jim Palmer:
Excellent. Well, thank you again for your time, Angela. And everybody, you'll be receiving a CD of this call in a few weeks with the January newsletter. Our next Gold call is Wednesday, December 17th. I will be sending you e-mail reminders about that. And, again, next month I'm going to spend the entire call answering your questions. So please e-mail me at jim@thenewsletterguru.com. That's jim@thenewsletterguru.com.

Remember folks, great newsletters are sales letters in disguise. So go out and sell something!

Until next time, this is Jim Palmer, The Newsletter Guru, and I look forward to sharing this time with you again next month. Good night, Angela, and good night everybody.

Angela Megasko:
Thanks, Jim.

Free Money-Making Video Reveals How To Achieve Higher Levels of Success Faster!

PLUS – Free Report Shows You How To Boost Your Profits And Get and Keep More Customers for Life!

Are your customers not staying around as long as you'd like? Can you count the number of referrals you get on one hand? Are you constantly searching for more new customers to replace the ones that leave? Well, I have the answers you need and I want to give you three free gifts just for visiting my Web site!

1. A free copy of my wildly popular report, Don't Be a Newsletter Pansy aka Use Newsletters and Grow Rich. In this report I'll show you how easy it is to get and keep more customers, dramatically boost your profits by increasing your repeat business and get more new customers by way of referrals.

2. I'm also going to share a video with you where I reveal an incredibly powerful business growth strategy that a highly successful mentor once shared with me. This strategy, The Power of Zero, has helped me more than double the size of my business in less than two years.

3. You'll also receive the first two chapters to my hit book, *The Magic of Newsletter Marketing*.

www.TheNewsletterGuru.com